GREAT EXPECTATIONS

ADAPTED FROM DICKENS' NOVEL
BY BARBARA FIELD

DRAMATISTS
PLAY SERVICE
INC.

GREAT EXPECTATIONS
Copyright © 1984, Barbara Field

All Rights Reserved

CAUTION: Professionals and amateurs are hereby warned that performance of GREAT EXPECTATIONS is subject to a royalty. It is fully protected under the copyright laws of the United States of America, and of all countries covered by the International Copyright Union (including the Dominion of Canada and the rest of the British Commonwealth), and of all countries covered by the Pan-American Copyright Convention, the Universal Copyright Convention, the Berne Convention, and of all countries with which the United States has reciprocal copyright relations. All rights, including professional/amateur stage rights, motion picture, recitation, lecturing, public reading, radio broadcasting, television, video or sound recording, all other forms of mechanical or electronic reproduction, such as CD-ROM, CD-I, DVD, information storage and retrieval systems and photocopying, and the rights of translation into foreign languages, are strictly reserved. Particular emphasis is placed upon the matter of readings, permission for which must be secured from the Author's agent in writing.

The stage performance rights in GREAT EXPECTATIONS (other than first class rights) are controlled exclusively by DRAMATISTS PLAY SERVICE, INC., 440 Park Avenue South, New York, NY 10016. No professional or non-professional performance of the Play (excluding first class professional performance) may be given without obtaining in advance the written permission of DRAMATISTS PLAY SERVICE, INC., and paying the requisite fee.

Inquiries concerning all other rights should be addressed to Berman, Boals and Flynn, 208 West 30th Street, Suite 401, New York, NY 10001. Attn: Judy Boals.

SPECIAL NOTE
Anyone receiving permission to produce GREAT EXPECTATIONS is required to give credit to the Author as sole and exclusive Author of the Play on the title page of all programs distributed in connection with performances of the Play and in all instances in which the title of the Play appears for purposes of advertising, publicizing or otherwise exploiting the Play and/or a production thereof. The name of the Author must appear on a separate line, in which no other name appears, immediately beneath the title and in size of type equal to 50% of the size of the largest, most prominent letter used for the title of the Play. No person, firm or entity may receive credit larger or more prominent than that accorded the Author.

SPECIAL NOTE ON MUSIC
Copies of original music tapes for use with GREAT EXPECTATIONS are availbable by arrangement with Berman, Boals and Flynn, 208 West 30th Street, Suite 401, New York, NY 10001.

To The Memory Of My Father
Harry Field

GREAT EXPECTATIONS was first presented by The Seattle Children's Theatre at the Poncho Theatre, in Seattle, Washington, on September 30, 1983. It was directed by Richard Edwards; the set design was by Bill Forrester; costume design was by Sheryl Collins; lighting design was by Lee DeLorme; the sound design was by Lindsay Smith; and the original music was composed and performed by Joseph Seserko. The cast was as follows:

```
YOUNG PIP ....................... Jonathan Bridgman/
                                  Isaac Benjamin Sterling
MAGWITCH ............................. Robert I. Lee
JOE GARGERY/AGED PARENT/PORTER/
   PRISON DOCTOR ...................... John Pribyl
MRS. JOE/MOLLY ...................... Mary Thielen
PUMBLECHOOK/WEMMICK/DRUMMLE . Todd Moore
LIEUTENANT/TAILOR/
   HERBERT POCKET .................... Geoffrey Alm
JAGGERS/COMPEYSON .................... Rex Allen
ESTELLA .......................... Katherine Kramer
MISS HAVISHAM/MISS SKIFFINS ..... Barbara McKean
BIDDY/CLARA ..................... Michelle Blackmon
YOUNG HERBERT POCKET ........... Joshua Ramsell/
                                  Jason Tanner
PIP ................................... Brett Keogh
JOE'S BOY ............................ Mark Branom
```

ABOUT THE AUTHOR

Barbara Field was the literary manager at the Guthrie Theater from 1974 through 1981. For that theatre she adapted Gogol's MARRIAGE, Bulgakov's MONSIEUR DE MOLIERE, Ghelderode's PANTAGLEIZE, and Dumas' CAMILLE. Other works include THE RENAISSANCE OF BARNABE BARNES, MATRIX, COMING OF AGE, PEN, and THE EDUCATION OF PAUL BUNYAN, plus the one-act scripts VISITING ANGELS, MATERIA MEDICA, and PERSON TO PERSON — the latter commissioned by the Actors Theatre of Louisville. Her NEUTRAL COUNTRIES was a co-winner of the 1983 Great American Play Contest at the Actors Theatre of Louisville and was produced there during the theatre's Festival that season.

Ms. Field has also authored an opera libretto, ROSINA, written with composer Hiram Titus which was commissioned and performed by the Minnesota Opera Company in 1981.

In 1976 and 1979, she was playwright-in-residence at the O'Neill National Playwrights Conference. She is co-founder and an active member of the Playwrights' Lab in Minneapolis.

THE COMPANY: SIX MEN, FOUR WOMEN, TWO BOYS, ONE GIRL, TO DOUBLE AS FOLLOWS:

Young Pip* Joe's boy	Young Herbert Stable Boy	Young Estella Barmaid
Pip Soldier	Herbert Pocket Lieutenant Tailor	Wemmick Pumblechook Bentley Drummle
Jaggers Compeyson** Clergyman	Joe Gargery Aged Parent Porter Prison Doctor	Magwitch A Pocket
Miss Havisham Miss Skiffins	Estella	Biddy Clara Barley A Pocket
Mrs. Joe Gargery Molly A Pocket		

*Young Pip's last scene takes place when he is told that he must apprentice himself to Joe. Adult Pip's first scene is at the Three Jolly Bargemen, page 26.

**The actor playing Jaggers can double as Compeyson, except for a few non-speaking crossovers in Act II. Since the character is heavily muffled, other actors may take turns at Compeyson during these scenes.

The children's roles, Pip, Herbert and Estella, may also be played by the actors who perform the same roles as adults.

ABOUT THE NARRATION:

The premise of this adaptation is that *all* of the actors tell the story; it is a shared effort in storytelling. Narration is assigned at the director's discretion. Narrating actors may be solitary and removed, may be part of the scene, or may be narrating while assisting in a scene change.

One interesting choice is to let narration *about* a particular character be spoken by the actor playing that role. For example (bottom of page 79), another member of the company can speak the line "The next morning early, after fortifying themselves with . . .", etc. But Pip might take the line, "Pip was puzzled."

There are over fifty scenes in this adaptation in more than a dozen locales. *It is imperative that scene changes take no more time than the narrative dialogue that accompanies them takes to deliver.*

The set is a neutral platform, with upstage scaffolding. This scaffolding performs several functions:

1. A (movable) part of it must become Miss Havisham's iron garden gate, allowing entrances from behind the scaffolding onto the stage.
2. It must contain a couple of functioning prop shelves for the actors to use.
3. If possible, the scaffolding should contain an upper level, with visible stairs.

There should also be one or two smallish wagons, which can be preset offstage with the few big set-pieces (Miss Havisham's table with the bride cake, for instance), then wheeled onstage either by actors or mechanically. Chairs can be hung on pegs at the sides of the stage or on the scaffolding. In any case, the furniture used should be as spare as possible, and should be manipulated rapidly.

The Thames river scenes have been written with a large map on the Thames estuary in mind — to be used on the floor if the stage is raked. Model boats manipulated by actors can travel on the map. The actors provide, in effect, a kind of voice-over for the action.

With one or two obvious exceptions, costume changes should be minimal.

Responsibility for most sound effects should also belong to the acting company, who can ring all the bells, make the rural sounds, etc., in view of the audience.

The premise on which this adaptation stands is that simple, honest storytelling and open use of the stage *as a stage* will be more effective than any literal-minded or realistic set.

GREAT EXPECTATIONS

ACT ONE

The entire company is assembled onstage, except for the actor playing Magwitch, who is already hiding behind the tombstone.

NARRATION.
His family name being Pirrip and his own name being Philip, in the beginning the boy could make of both names nothing longer than . . . Pip.

So he called himself Pip,

And came to be called Pip.

The family name, Pirrip, he had on the authority of a certain tombstone, his father's,

And on the authority of his older sister, Mrs. Joe Gargery,

Who was married to the town blacksmith.

They lived in the marsh country of Kent, where the Thames ran down to the sea.

In that dark, flat wilderness was a village churchyard where, one day, Pip found his parents.

Churchyard. A Few Tombstones. Pip kneels in front of one of them, reads haltingly.

PIP. "Philip Pirrip, late of this parish." (*Pause.*) "Also Georgiana, wife of the above . . ."
NARRATION. The boy, a small bundle of shivers, began to cry, when—(*Magwitch pops up from behind a tombstone.*)
MAGWITCH. Keep still, you little devil, or I'll cut your throat!

PIP. Oh don't, sir!
MAGWITCH. Tell us your name quick, then!
PIP. Pip, sir. (*Magwitch lifts him abruptly, sets him atop the stone, searches him. He finds a crust of bread, which he gnaws.*)
MAGWITCH. Lookee here, then — where's your mother?
PIP. There, sir. (*Magwitch starts.*) There — "Also Georgiana". That's my mother.
MAGWITCH. Hah. And that's your father, alonger your mother?
PIP. Yes, sir. "Late of this parish."
MAGWITCH. Hah. And who d'ye live with now, supposin' I kindly let you live, which I haven't made up my mind about?
PIP. My sister, Mrs. Joe Gargery. She's wife to the blacksmith.
MAGWITCH. Blacksmith, eh? (*He looks down at his leg irons.*) Lookee here: the question being whether or not you're to be let live — you know what a file is?
PIP. Yes, sir.
MAGWITCH. And you know what wittles is?
PIP. Wittles is food, sir.
MAGWITCH. You bring me a file and you bring me some wittles, or I'll have your heart and liver out. Bring 'em tomorrow at dawn — and don't say a word about having seen me — and I'll let you live. (*Pip nods.*) But mind, I'm not alone, if you're thinking that. No indeed, there's a young man hid with me, in comparison with which young man *I* am an angel. So you must do as I tell you.
PIP. Yes, sir.
MAGWITCH. (*Pulls out a little Bible.*) Swear — say "Lord strike me dead if I don't."
PIP. "Lord strike me dead if I don't." (*Magwitch gives him a dismissing nod. The boy backs away, then bolts. Magwitch huddles by the tombstone.*)

The Forge Kitchen.

NARRATION.
Pip's sister, Mrs. Joe Gargery, was more than twenty years older than the boy.

She had established a great reputation as a foster parent, because she had brought the boy up *by hand*.
(*As Pip races in, she slaps him.*)

She was neither a good-looking woman, nor a cheerful one.
(*Joe steps in to protect Pip.*)

Pip had the impression that she must have made Joe Gargery marry her *by hand,* too.
(*She slaps Joe, as well.*)

MRS. JOE. Where've you been, young monkey? I'm worn away with fret and fright over you.

PIP. I've only been to the churchyard.

MRS. JOE. Churchyard! If it weren't for me you'd have been in the churchyard long ago. Bad enough being a blacksmith's wife, and him a Gargery, without being your mother as well. You'll drive *me* to the churchyard one of these days, between the two of you. (*As she talks, she butters a slice of bread, hands it to Pip with another slap. He takes a bite, then when she isn't looking, he secretes the rest in his pocket. Joe notices, however. Mrs. Joe turns to Pip.*) Where's your bread? Did you swallow it whole? This boy has the manners of a swine!

JOE. Oh no, my dear, I don't think he —

MRS. JOE. Don't my dear me! I'm not your dear. (*She hands Pip a slate, some chalk.*)

NARRATION. Pip felt little tenderness of conscience toward his sister. But Joe he loved. (*Joe watches Pip writing laboriously on the slate.*)

JOE. I say, Pip, old chap, what a scholar you are!

PIP. I'd like to be. (*He writes.*) How do you spell Gargery?

JOE. I don't spell it at all.

PIP. But supposing you did?

JOE. It cannot be supposed — though I am oncommon fond of reading.

PIP. Are you, Joe? I didn't know that.

JOE. Oncommon — give me a good book and I ask nothin' better.

PIP. (*Pause.*) Did you ever go to school?

JOE. My father, he were given to drink, Pip; and whenever he were overtook with drink, he'd beat my mother and me, most onmerciful. We ran away a time or two, and my mother would find a job. "Joe," she'd say, "now you shall have some schooling, please God." And so I'd start school. But my father was such a good-hearted man, he couldn't bear to live without us, so he'd hunt us down and drag us home. Then he'd beat us up again to show how he'd missed us. Which you see, Pip, were a serious drawback to my learning. (*Mrs. Joe takes Pip's slate away.*)

MRS. JOE. Time for bed, boy. (*She gives him a slap for good measure.*)

JOE. Time for bed, Pip, old chap. (*Whispers.*) Your sister is much given to government, which I meantersay the government of you and myself. (*He hugs Pip. There is a distant boom of a cannon.*)

MRS. JOE. Hark, the guns.

JOE. Ay. It must be another conwict off, eh?

PIP. Off?

MRS. JOE. Escaped, escaped.

PIP. Please, Joe, where's the shooting come from?

MRS. JOE. Ask no questions, you'll be told no lies.

JOE. It comes from the Hulks, Pip, old chap.

PIP. Please, Joe, what's the Hulks?

MRS. JOE. This boy! Answer one question and he'll ask a dozen more!

JOE. Hulks is prison ships.

PIP. And please, Joe —

MRS. JOE. No more! Time for bed! Bed! Bed! Bed!

NARRATION.

Conscience is a dreadful thing when it accuses a boy.

Pip labored with the thought that he was to become a thief the next morning . . .

Which was Christmas Day.
    (*The cannon booms.*)

Pip scarcely slept that night.

When pale dawn came he crept into the forge where he stole a file, and thence into the pantry where he stole a loaf of bread,

Some brandy,

And a beautiful, round firm pork pie.

As he ran toward the marshes, the mist, the wind, the very cattle in the field seemed to accuse him.

Stop thief! Stop that boy!

> *The Churchyard. Pip runs toward the convict, whose back is to Pip. The man turns at Pip's whistle—but it is not the same man! Both gasp, then the man runs off. Pip empties his pockets, then Magwitch appears. He grabs the brandy.*

MAGWITCH. What's in the bottle, boy?
PIP. Brandy. (*Magwitch stuffs the food into his mouth. He shivers as he eats.*) I think you've caught a chill, sir.
MAGWITCH. I'm much of your opinion, boy. (*He pauses, listens.*) You brought no one with you? (*Pip shakes his head.*) I believe you. You'd be a mean young hound if you could help hunt down a wretched warmint like me, eh? (*Pip watches him eat.*)
PIP. I'm glad you enjoy your food, sir.
MAGWITCH. Thankee, boy, I do.
PIP. But I'm afraid you haven't left much for him.
MAGWITCH. Who's him?
PIP. That young man you spoke of, who's with you.
MAGWITCH. Oh, *him*. (*He grins.*) He don't want no wittles.
PIP. He looked as if he did—
MAGWITCH. —Looked? When? (*He rises.*)
PIP. Just now.
MAGWITCH. —Where?!
PIP. Right here, a few minutes ago. I thought it was you—he wore gray, like you, and he wore . . . he had the same reason for wanting a file. He ran away.
MAGWITCH. Did he have a scar on his face?
PIP. (*Nods.*) Here.
MAGWITCH. Give us that file, boy. (*Magwitch starts to file his leg irons.*) And they ye'd best go—they'll be missing you! (*Pip nods, then runs off.*)
NARRATION.
As Pip ran home, he could still hear the file sawing away at the convict's fetters.

He fully expected to find a constable waiting to arrest him when he got home.

But there was only Mrs. Joe, readying the house for Christmas dinner.

The Forge Kitchen.

MRS. JOE. —And where the deuce ha' you been now? Company's expected!
PIP. I was . . . down to hear the carolers. (*She gives him a crack on the head.*)
JOE. Merry Christmas, Pip, old chap.
NARRATION.
Dinner was set for half-past one. There was one guest . . .

Mr. Pumblechook, wealthy seed-and-corn merchant in the nearby town.

He was Joe's uncle, but he was Mrs. Joe's ally.
PUMBLECHOOK. Mrs. Joe, I have brought you a bottle of sherry wine, and I have brought you a bottle of port wine, in honor of the Day.
MRS. JOE. You was ever the soul of generosity, Uncle. (*They sit at table. She cuffs Pip.*) Stop fidgeting, boy—he wriggles as if he had a guilty conscience.
PUMBLECHOOK. Then he must indeed have one. Boys, Joseph—a bad lot!
MRS. JOE. Will you say the blessing, Uncle Pumblechook?
PUMBLECHOOK. For that which we are about to receive, may the Lord make us truly thankful.
ALL. Amen.
PUMBLECHOOK. D'you hear that, boy? Be ever thankful to them what has brought you up by hand.
PIP. Yes, sir.
PUMBLECHOOK. Joseph, why is it the young are never thankful? I declare, boys are naturally wicious!
MRS. JOE. Too true, Uncle Pumblechook.
JOE. Have some gravy, Pip? (*He ladles it onto Pip's plate.*)
PUMBLECHOOK. Not too much—the Lord invented the pig

as an example of gluttony to the young. (*To Mrs. Joe.*) He's no end of trouble to you, is he, ma'am?
MRS. JOE. Trouble? You cannot know what trouble he's been.
JOE. More gravy, Pip old fellow, old chap, old friend?
PUMBLECHOOK. I suppose this boy will be apprenticed to you, soon, Joseph?
MRS. JOE. Not for another year. Till then he'll eat me out of house and home — but I'm forgetting! I've a delicious pork pie, yet! (*Pip drops his fork.*)
PUMBLECHOOK. Ah, pork pie! A morcel of pie would lay atop any dinner you might mention, and do no harm, eh?
MRS. JOE. I'll just go fetch it. (*She goes. Pip rises in terror, rushes to the front door to escape. Simultaneously, a sharp knock at the door, and a scream from Mrs. Joe. At the door, Pip is confronted by a pair of handcuffs, held by a soldier.*)

LIEUTENANT. Hello, young fellow —
Does the blacksmith live here?

MRS. JOE. (*Off.*)

Stop! Stop, thief, my pie — it's been stolen.

Well?
PUMBLECHOOK. This is the blacksmith's, yes.
LIEUTENANT. Sorry to disturb your Christmas dinner —
PUMBLECHOOK. Think nothing of it, my good man.
LIEUTENANT. — But we've caught two convicts, and need these irons repaired. Can you do it?
PUMBLECHOOK. Not me, him. He's the smith. Certainly he can do it. (*Mrs. Joe enters, distraught.*)
MRS. JOE. My pork pie — it's gone —
LIEUTENANT. (*To Joe.*) By the way, is this your file?
JOE. (*Examines it.*) Which it are!
LIEUTENANT. It was found in the churchyard —
MRS. JOE. Thieves, thieves . . . (*Pumblechook is already pouring port wine down her throat.*)

NARRATION.
Christmas dinner was over.

When Pip arrived at the boat landing with Joe, he recognized *his* convict — and the other, with the scarred face.

> (*The convicts glare at each other. The Lieutenant takes the handcuffs from Joe, snaps them on Magwitch. The other man, Compeyson, lunges at Magwitch, is pulled off by soldiers.*)

MAGWITCH. I took 'im! I caught the villain! I turned 'im in, don't forget.

COMPEYSON. This man — this man has tried to murder me!

MAGWITCH. See what a villain he is — look at his eyes! Don't forget, I caught 'im for ye! (*Magwitch turns, notices Pip. Pip gives him a tiny shake of the head.*) I wish ter say something respectin' this escape. It may prevent some persons from lying under suspicion alonger me.

LIEUTENANT. You'll have plenty of chance later —

MAGWITCH. — But this is a separate matter. I stole some wittles up in the willage yonder. Likewise a file —

JOE. Halloa, Pip?

MAGWITCH. And some liquor. And a pie. (*To Joe.*) Sorry to say, I've eat your pie.

JOE. God knows you're welcome to it, as far as it was ever mine. We don't know what you have done, but we wouldn't have you starved to death for it, poor miserable fellow. Would us, Pip? (*Pip shakes his head. The Lieutenant calls out, "ready! move!" The prisoners are marched off, Magwitch stops, turns back. He and Pip stare at each other for a moment, then he goes off. Darkness.*)

The Forge Kitchen.

NARRATION.
It was not long after the incident on the marsh that Mrs. Joe returned home in the company of Mr. Pumblechook, in a state of rare excitement.

> (*Joe smoking his pipe in a chair, Pip on the floor beside him. Mrs. Joe and Pumblechook burst in.*)

MRS. JOE. If this boy ain't grateful this night, he never will be! (*Pip tries to look grateful.*) It's only to be hoped she won't fill his head with silly ideas.

PUMBLECHOOK. I doubt it. She knows better.

JOE. Which someone mentioned a *she?*

MRS. JOE. Unless you call Miss Havisham a he—
JOE. Miss Havisham? That odd, solitary lady in the town?
MRS. JOE. She wants this boy to go play there. Of course he's going—and he'd better play, or I'll work him! (*She cracks Pip on the head.*)
JOE. Well, to be sure. I wonder how she come to know Pip?
MRS. JOE. Noodle—who says she knows him? (*She cracks Joe on the head.*) Couldn't she ask Uncle Pumblechook if he knew of a boy to go play there? Isn't it barely possible that Uncle Pumblechook may be a tenant of hers; and might he go there to pay his rent? And couldn't Uncle, out of the goodness of his heart, mention this boy here—to whom I have ever been a willing slave?
PUMBLECHOOK. Now, Joseph, you know the case.
MRS. JOE. No, Uncle, Joseph does not know the case. (*To Joe.*) For you do not know that Uncle, aware that this boy's fortune might be made by Miss Havisham, has offered to deliver Pip to her tomorrow, with his own hands! What do you say to that?
JOE. (*Mystified.*) Thankee kindly, Uncle Pumblechook.
PUMBLECHOOK. My duty, Joseph. (*To Pip.*) Boy, be ever grateful to those what brought you up by hand. (*He gives Pip a box on the ear.*)
NARRATION.
Miss Havisham's house was of dismal bricks.

Most of its windows were boarded up.

There was a tall iron gate before which Mr. Pumblechook and Pip appeared at ten the next morning.

> *Miss Havisham's. The garden; then a room. Mr. Pumblechook rings the bell.*

PUMBLECHOOK. Right on the dot of ten, boy.
PIP. No sir, I believe we're early. See, her big tower clock says twenty to nine.
PUMBLECHOOK. It must have stopped. My timepiece is always correct. (*Estella appears.*)
ESTELLA. What name?

PUMBLECHOOK. Pumblechook.
ESTELLA. Quite right. (*She unlocks the gate. Pumblechook pushes Pip through.*)
PUMBLECHOOK. This is Pip.
ESTELLA. This is Pip, is it? Come in, Pip. (*Pumblechook tries to follow.*) Do you wish to see Miss Havisham?
PUMBLECHOOK. I'm sure Miss Havisham wishes to see me.
ESTELLA. Ah, but you see, she don't. (*She shuts the gate in his face, leads Pip on.*) Don't loiter, boy.
NARRATION.
Although she was about Pip's age, to him she seemed years older —

Being beautiful and self-possessed —

And being a girl.
> (*She leads Pip upward, with a candle in her hand. She knocks. A voice says "come in." Estella gestures Pip into the room, then leaves. It is dark. There is a banquet table with a huge cake. Miss Havisham is seated before it.*)

HAVISHAM. Who is it?
PIP. Pip, ma'am.
HAVISHAM. Pip?
PIP. Mr. Pumblechook's boy, ma'am. Come to play.
HAVISHAM. Come nearer, let me look at you. Come closer.
NARRATION.
Once Pip had been taken to see a waxwork at a fair.

Once he had been taken to an old church to see a skeleton in the ashes of a rich robe, which had been dug out of a vault.

Now waxwork and skeleton seemed to have dark eyes that moved, and looked at him.
HAVISHAM. Come closer. Ah, you are not afraid of a woman who has never seen the sun since you were born?
PIP. . . . No.
HAVISHAM. You know what I touch here?
PIP. Your heart.
HAVISHAM. Broken. (*Pause.*) I am tired. I want diversion. Play. (*Pip does not move.*) I sometimes have sick fancies; and I

have a sick fancy that I'd like to see someone play. Play. Play, play! (*Pip does not move.*) Are you so sullen and obstinate?
PIP. I'm very sorry, but I can't play just now. I would if I could, but it's all so new here . . . so strange and fine and . . . melancholy.
HAVISHAM. So new to him, so old to me; so strange to him, so familiar to me; so melancholy to us both. (*Estella enters.*) Let me see you play cards with this boy.
ESTELLA. With this boy!? Why, he's nothing but a common laboring boy!
HAVISHAM. (*Aside to Estella.*) Well? You can break his heart.
ESTELLA. What do you play, boy?
PIP. Only "Beggar My Neighbor", miss. (*Estella brings out a deck of cards, deals. They play. Pip drops some cards.*)
ESTELLA. He's stupid and clumsy — look at his hands, so coarse! (*They play.*)
HAVISHAM. (*To Pip.*) You say nothing of her. What do you think of her, tell me in my ear.
PIP. (*Whispers.*) I think she is very proud.
HAVISHAM. Anything else?
PIP. I think she is very pretty.
HAVISHAM. Anything else?
PIP. I think she is very insulting and I'd like to go home.
HAVISHAM. You may go soon. Finish the game. (*They play.*)
NARRATION.
The girl won. Her name was Estella.

Pip was asked to return the next week.

Estella took the candle and led him out.
ESTELLA. (*Going.*) You're crude. You're clumsy. Your boots are ugly!
NARRATION.
The girl saw tears spring to Pip's eyes.

Pip saw her quick delight at having been the cause of them.

And for the first time, he was bitterly aware that life had been unjust to him.

He quickly dried his eyes so she would not catch him weeping.
ESTELLA. Why don't you cry again, boy?

PIP. Because I don't want to.
ESTELLA. Yes you do. You cried before, and you'll cry again —
NARRATION.
Pip headed for home with the shameful knowledge that his hands were coarse and his boots were ugly,

And that he was much more ignorant than he had thought himself the night before.

The Forge Kitchen.
Pumblechook, Mrs. Joe and Joe wait eagerly. Pip enters.

PUMBLECHOOK. Well, boy? How did you get on?
PIP. Pretty well, sir.
PUMBLECHOOK. "Pretty well?" Tell us what you mean by pretty well, boy.
PIP. I mean pretty well.
PUMBLECHOOK. And what is she like?
PIP. Very tall and fat.
MRS. JOE. Is she, Uncle? (*Pause. Pumblechook nods vaguely.*)
PUMBLECHOOK. Now, tell us what she was doing when you went in?
PIP. She was sitting in a big black velvet coach. (*His listeners are amazed. Pip smiles.*) Miss Estella handed her wine and cake, into the coach. We all had wine and cake — on golden plates! (*Astonished pause.*)
PUMBLECHOOK. Was anyone else there?
PIP. Four black dogs.
PUMBLECHOOK. Large or small?
PIP. Immense!
PUMBLECHOOK. That's the truth of it, ma'am, I've seen it myself the times I've called on her. (*He bows, exits with Mrs. Joe. Pip whistles a tune to himself.*)
NARRATION. After Mr. Pumblechook departed, Pip — or his conscience — sought out Joe.
PIP. It was all lies, Joe.
JOE. Really? The black velvet coach was a lie?
PIP. Yes.
JOE. Even the golden plates?

PIP. I wish my boots weren't so thick, Joe, I wish—(*He throws his arms around Joe, buries his face in Joe's shoulder.*)
NARRATION. He told Joe how miserable he'd been made to feel, by Uncle Pumblechook and Mrs. Joe, and by the very beautiful young lady who had called him common.
JOE. One thing, Pip, lies is lies and you mustn't tell any more of 'em. That ain't the way to stop bein' common. As for that, in some ways you're most oncommon. You're oncommon small. You're an oncommon scholar.
PIP. I'm not, I'm ignorant and clumsy.
JOE. Pip? Even the four black dogs was lies?

NARRATION.
Although Pip could not improve the quality of his boots, he set about to remedy the quality of his education by taking lessons from Mr. Pumblechook's great-aunt's grand-niece—

Biddy—who lived in the neighborhood.
BIDDY. (*Holds up a slate to Pip.*) Six times four.
PIP. Twenty-four.
BIDDY. Seven times four?
PIP. Twenty-eight.
BIDDY. Eight times four? (*A pause. Pip isn't sure of the answer and, to tell the truth, neither is Biddy.*)
PIP. Thirty-four? (*She nods approval.*)
NARRATION. And a week later he returned to Miss Havisham's at the appointed hour.

Miss Havisham's. The garden, then a room.

ESTELLA. Follow me, boy. Well?
PIP. Well, miss?
ESTELLA. Am I pretty?
PIP. Very.
ESTELLA. Am I insulting?
PIP. Not so much as you were last time.

ESTELLA. No? (*She slaps his face.*) Coarse little monster, why don't you cry?
PIP. I'll never cry for you again. (*As they cross, they pass Mr. Jaggers coming from the other direction.*)
NARRATION. As Estella led him through the gloomy house, they encountered a singular-looking gentleman coming toward them.
JAGGERS. Well, well, what have we here?
ESTELLA. A boy.
JAGGERS. Boy of the neighborhood?
PIP. Yes, sir.
JAGGERS. How d'you come to be here?
ESTELLA. Miss Havisham sent for him, sir.
JAGGERS. Well, behave yourself. I've a pretty large experience of boys, and you're a bad set of fellows. Behave! (*He continues out. Estella and Pip enter Miss Havisham's room.*)
HAVISHAM. So, the days have worn away, have they? A week. Are you ready to play?
PIP. I don't think so, ma'am.
HAVISHAM. Are you willing to work, then? (*Pip nods. She takes his arm, leans against his shoulder.*) Help me to walk, boy. (*They circle the table.*) This is where I shall be laid when I am dead. (*She points with her stick.*) What do you think that is?
PIP. I cannot guess.
HAVISHAM. It's a great cake. A bride-cake. Mine.
PIP. There are mice in it, ma'am.
HAVISHAM. Yes. This cake and I have worn away together, and sharper teeth have gnawed at me.
NARRATION. Breathing the heavy air that brooded in the room, Pip suddenly had an alarming fancy that all was decaying—that even he and Estella might presently begin to decay.
HAVISHAM. Now you must play at cards. (*Estella gets the deck.*) Is she not pretty, Pip? (*Pip sighs, nods. Estella deals.*)
NARRATION.
And so the visits ran, with little to distinguish one
from another.

Estella always won at cards.

Once, some relations called upon Miss Havisham.
A POCKET. How well you look, ma'am.

A POCKET. Happy birthday, cousin—
A POCKET. —And many happy returns of the day.
HAVISHAM. You see, Pip? The vultures have descended again, my Pocket relations. But the Pockets shall not have a penny of mine, never! You may go, Pip.
NARRATION.
Pip was all too glad to take his leave.

He was about to let himself out by the garden gate,
when he was stopped by a pale young gentleman.
 (*Young Herbert appears, munching an apple.*)
YOUNG HERBERT. Halloa, young fellow. Who let you in?
PIP. Miss Estella.
YOUNG HERBERT. (*Pleasantly.*) Do you want to fight? Come on. (*He tosses the apple over his shoulder, strips off his cap, jacket and shirt.*) I ought to give you a reason for fighting. There— (*He claps his hands together under Pip's nose, gently pulls his hair. He dances around Pip, fists doubled.*) Standard rules, is that agreeable? (*Pip nods. Herbert dances around, throwing punches which miss Pip. Pip finally gets one off, and it levels Herbert. Estella peeps out to watch.*)
PIP. Oh dear, I'm sorry—
YOUNG HERBERT. Think nothing of it, young fellow! (*He jumps to his feet, squeezes a sponge of water over his head, dances around again. Pip lands another punch, Herbert falls.*)
PIP. Oh, look, I'm really so sorry, I—
YOUNG HERBERT. Perfectly all right. (*He gets up, picks up the sponge, throws it.*) See, I'm throwing in the sponge. That means you've won. (*He offers his hand. They shake.*)
PIP. Can I help you?
YOUNG HERBERT. No thankee, I'm fine. (*He picks up his jacket and cap. As he goes off, Estella passes him, sticks out her tongue. He shrugs, leaves. Pip stares after him. Estella comes to him.*)
ESTELLA. You may kiss me, if you like. (*He kisses her on the cheek, then, overwhelmed, he flees.*)

NARRATION.
If Pip could have told Joe about his strange visits—

If he could have unburdened himself about his love for Estella, or even about his fight with the pale young gentleman—

But of course he could not, for Joe's hands were coarser and his boots thicker than Pip's own!

So Pip confided in Biddy—it seemed natural to do so. He told her everything,

And Biddy had a deep concern in everything he told her.
    (*Pip and Biddy are strolling, sharing a piece of toffee.*)
PIP. Biddy, I want to be a gentleman.
BIDDY. Oh, I wouldn't if I was you, Pip.
PIP. I've my reasons for wanting it.
BIDDY. You know best, but wouldn't you be happier as you are?
PIP. I am not happy as I am! I am disgusted with my life.
BIDDY. That's a pity for you, isn't it?
PIP. I know. If I was half as fond of the forge as I was a year ago, life would be simpler. I could become Joe's partner someday. Who knows, perhaps I'd even keep company with you. I'd be good enough for *you,* wouldn't I, Biddy?
BIDDY. Oh yes, I am not over-particular. (*Pause.*) Is it Estella?
PIP. It's because of her I wish to be a gentleman.
BIDDY. Do you wish to be a gentleman to spite her or to win her?
PIP. I don't know. Biddy, I wish you could put me right.
BIDDY. I wish I could . . .

NARRATION.
But Biddy could not put Pip right.

Things went on in the same way. His dreams and discontent remained.

Time passed.

Finally, one day Miss Havisham looked at him crossly—
HAVISHAM. You are growing too tall! What is the name of that blacksmith of yours?
PIP. Joe Gargery, ma'am.
HAVISHAM. I shan't need you to come play here anymore.

So you'd better be apprenticed to Mr. Gargery at once.
PIP. But—
HAVISHAM. But what?
PIP. —I don't want to be a blacksmith! I'd rather come here!
HAVISHAM. It's all over, Pip. You're growing up. Estella is going abroad to school next week. Gargery is your master now. (*She glances at Estella, whispers to Pip.*) Does she grow prettier, Pip? Do you love her? Shall you miss her? (*Pip turns away, she crosses to Estella.*) Break their hearts, my pride and hope, break their hearts and have no mercy.

NARRATION.
Pip was indentured as apprentice blacksmith to Joe Gargery the following week.

Miss Havisham's parting gift of twenty-five pounds was cause for celebration in some quarters.
    (*Mr. Pumblechook and Mrs. Joe toast.*)

Pip did not celebrate. He had liked Joe's trade once,

But once was not now.

He was wretched.
    (*Sound of an anvil. Glow of a forge fire.*)

Nonetheless, Pip labored.

And Pip grew.

Always he would gaze into the fire at the forge and see Estella's face.

He heard her cruel laughter in the wind.

He was haunted by the fear that she would come home, witness his debasement, and despise him.

On the surface, however, Pip's life fell into a routine.

Days he worked with Joe at the forge. Evenings he became his own teacher—

For he had long outstripped Biddy in learning.

Once a year, on his birthday, he visited Miss Havisham.
HAVISHAM. Pip, is it? Has your birthday come round again? Ah, you're looking around for her, I see. Still abroad, educating for a lady . . . far out of reach and prettier than ever. Do you feel you have lost her?
NARRATION.
Time wrought other changes.

Mrs. Joe Gargery fell gravely ill, and lingered in a kind of twilight, tended by Biddy,

Who was more sweet-tempered and wholesome than ever.

Pip was now a young man, old enough to accompany Joe to the local public house of an evening.

And so, in the fourth year of his apprenticeship, on a Saturday night at the Three Jolly Bargemen. . . .

The Pub.
Pumblechook, Joe and Pip at a table. Jaggers sits at a distance, in the shadows. Others are also drinking. A barmaid serves. Pumblechook is reading from a newspaper.

PUMBLECHOOK. "The wictim is said to have spoken the name of the accused before he died, according to a witness for the prosecution. And medical testimony brought out during the third day of the trial by the prosecution points to—"
JAGGERS. I suppose you've settled the case to your satisfaction? (*Pumblechook peers into the shadows.*)
PUMBLECHOOK. Sir, without having the honor of your acquaintance, I *have*. The werdict should be "guilty."
JAGGERS. I thought as much. (*He rises.*) But the trial is not over, is it? You do admit that English law supposes each man to be innocent until he is proved—*proved*—guilty?
PUMBLECHOOK. Certainly I admit it, sir.
JAGGERS. And are you aware, or are you not aware, that none of the witnesses mentioned in that questionable journal you read has yet been cross-examined by the defense?

PUMBLECHOOK. Yes, but—
JAGGERS. I rest my case. (*He peers around the room.*) From information I have received, I've reason to believe there's a blacksmith among you by the name of Joseph Gargery. Which is the man?
PUMBLECHOOK. There is the man. What have you done, Joseph?
JAGGERS. And you have an apprentice who is commonly known as Pip—is he here?
PUMBLECHOOK. Aha! I knew that boy would come to no good!
JAGGERS. I wish a conference with you two—a private conference. (*The others drift away, grumbling.*) My name is Jaggers, and I am a lawyer in London. I'm pretty well known there. I've some unusual business to transact with you. (*Pip and Joe glance at each other.*) Know first that I act as the confidential agent of a client. It is his orders I follow, not my own. Having said that: Joseph Gargery, I've come with an offer to relieve you of this apprentice of yours.
JOE. Pip?
JAGGERS. Would you be willing to cancel his indentures, for his own good? (*Joe thinks, nods.*) You'd ask no money for doing so?
JOE. Lord forbid I should want anything for not standing in Pip's way.
JAGGERS. Good. Don't try to change your mind later. (*With great formality:*) The communication I have come to make is . . . that this young man has great expectations. (*Pip rises. He and Joe gape.*) I'm instructed to inform him that he will come into a handsome fortune; that he is to be immediately removed from his present sphere of life and from this place, that he is to be brought up as a gentleman—in a word, as befits a young man of great expectations. (*Joe and Pip stare wordlessly for a moment.*)
PIP. Joe—
JAGGERS. —Later. First, understand that the person from whom I take my instruction requests that you always bear the name of Pip. You've no objection, I daresay? Good. Secondly, *Mr.* Pip, the name of your benefactor—
PIP. —Miss Havisham—
JAGGERS. —the name of your benefactor must remain a

secret until that person chooses to reveal it. Do you accept this condition? Good. Good. I've already been given a sum of money for your education and maintenance. From now on, you will please consider me your guardian.
PIP. Thank you—
JAGGERS. —Don't bother to thank me, I am well-paid for my services, or I shouldn't render them. Now then, education: you wish a proper tutor, no doubt? Good. Have you a preference?
PIP. Well . . . I only know Biddy, that's Mr. Pumblechook's great-aunt's grand-niece—
JAGGERS. —Never mind, there's a man in London who might suit well enough, a Mr. Matthew Pocket.
PIP. Pocket—is he a cousin of Miss Havisham?
JAGGERS. Ah, you know the name. He is. When do you wish to come to London?
PIP. Soon-directly!
JAGGERS. Good. You'll need proper clothes—here is twenty guineas. You'll take the hackney coach up to London—it's a five-hour trip. Shall I look for you a week from tomorrow? Good. Well, Joseph Gargery, you look dumbfounded.
JOE. Which I am.
JAGGERS. It was understood you wanted nothing for yourself.
JOE. It were understood and it are understood and ever will be.
JAGGERS. But what if I was instructed to make you a present, as compensation for the loss of his services—?
JOE. —Pip is that hearty welcome to go free with his services to honor and fortune, as no words can tell him. But if you think as money can compensate me for the loss of the little child what—what come to the forge and . . . and . . . ever the best of friends. (*He WEEPS.*)
PIP. Oh, Joe, don't . . . I'm going to be a gentleman! (*Darkness.*)

NARRATION.
That night Pip sat alone in his little room at the forge, feeling sorrowful and strange that this first night of his bright fortune should be the loneliest he had ever known.

The next morning, things looked brighter —

Only seven days until his departure.

Seven *long* days.

But there was much to do. First he visited a tailor.
PIP. (*Rings Bell.*) I beg your pardon . . .
TAILOR. (*Unimpressed.*) I beg yours.
PIP. I am going to London.
TAILOR. What of it?
PIP. I shall need a suit of fashionable clothes. (*Pip drops coins one-by-one into the hand of the tailor, who becomes obsequious. During the following Pip goes behind a screen and changes his clothes as:*)
TAILOR. I beg your pardon, my dear sir. Fashionable clothes, is it? For London! You've come to the right place, you shall be quite correct, I assure you, quite the thing! Indeed, one might call you the "glass of fashion". We'll turn you out from top to toe as fine as any London gentleman could wish!
NARRATION. And thence, to Mr. Pumblechook's, to receive that great man's blessing.
PUMBLECHOOK. (*Raising a glass.*) Beloved friend, I give you joy in your good fortune. Well-deserved, well-deserved! And to think that I have been the humble instrument leading up to all this . . . is reward enough for me. So here's to you — I always knew you had it in you! And let us also drink thanks to Fortune — may she ever pick her favorites with equal judgement!
NARRATION. And thence to Miss Havisham's, with barely suppressed excitement . . . and gratitude. (*Pip emerges from behind the screen. His London suit is almost comical in its exaggeration of high fashion. It is de trop.*)
HAVISHAM. This is a grand figure, Pip.
PIP. Oh, ma'am, I have come into such good fortune!
HAVISHAM. I've learned of it from Mr. Jaggers. So, you've been adopted by a rich person, have you?
PIP. Yes, Miss Havisham.
HAVISHAM. Not named?
PIP. Not named.
HAVISHAM. You've a promising career before you. Deserve it! You're always to keep the name of Pip, you know? (*He nods.*)

Goodbye then, Pip. (*She puts out her hand, he kisses it clumsily.*)
NARRATION. Finally, the morning of his departure dawned.

The Forge Kitchen.

PIP. You may be sure, dear Joe, I shall never forget you.
JOE. Ay, old chap, I'm sure of that.
PIP. I always dreamed of being a gentleman.
JOE. Did you? Astonishing! Now me, I'm an awful dull fellow. I'm only master in my own trade, but . . . ever the best of friends— (*He flees in tears.*)
PIP. (*To Biddy.*) You will help Joe on, won't you?
BIDDY. How help him on?
PIP. Joe's a dear fellow, the dearest that ever lived, but he's backward in some things, Biddy . . . like learning and manners.
BIDDY. Won't his manners do, then?
PIP. They do well enough here, but if I were to bring him to London when I come into my property—
BIDDY. —And don't you think he knows that? Pip, Pip . . .
PIP. Well?
BIDDY. Have you never considered his pride?
PIP. His pride? Whatever do you mean? You sound almost envious—
BIDDY. If you have the heart to think so! Can't you see, Joe is too proud and too wise to let anyone remove him from a place he fills with dignity—(*Joe enters, blowing his nose.*)
JOE. It's time for the coach, Pip.
PIP. Well then. (*He picks up his valise.*)
JOE. I'll come wisit you in London, old chap, and then—wot larks, eh? Wot larks we'll have!
PIP. Goodbye, Biddy. (*He kisses her cheek.*) Dear Joe—(*Joe grabs Pip's hat, throws it up in the air, to hide his tears.*)
JOE. Hoorar! Hoorar! (*With waves and cheers, the "coach" departs for London.*)

NARRATION.
When his coach finally left the village behind, Pip wept.

Heaven knows we need never be ashamed of our tears,
for they are the rain on the blinding dust of earth,
overlaying our hard hearts.

Pip felt better after he had cried—

More aware of his own ingratitude,

Sorrier,

Gentler.

But by now it was too late to turn back to Joe, so
he traveled forward.

The mists slowly rose and the world lay spread before him.

And suddenly there was—
COACHMAN. London!
PIP. London! (*Pip climbs off the "coach", clutching his valise. He stares around him at the crowd.*)
NARRATION. Not far from the great dome of St. Paul's, in the very shadow of Newgate Prison, Pip alighted and stood before an ugly stone building.

Jaggers's Office.
Wemmick appears at Pip's knock. Jaggers is inside the room, washing his hands. He pours water from a pitcher into a basin, as:

PIP. Is Mr. Jaggers in? (*Wemmick pulls him inside.*)
WEMMICK. Am I addressing Mr. Pip? He's been expecting you. I'm Wemmick, Mr. Jaggers's clerk. (*He leads Pip to Jaggers.*)
JAGGERS. Well, Mr. Pip, London, eh?
PIP. Yes, sir.
JAGGERS. I've made arrangements for you to stay at Barnard's Inn. You'll share young Mr. Pocket's apartments.
PIP. My tutor?
JAGGERS. His son. I've sent over some furniture for you. And here's a list of tradesmen where you may run up bills. And you will, you will—you'll drown in debt before the year is out, I'm

sure, but that's no fault of mine, is it? Good. Wemmick, take him over to Barnard's Inn, will you? I must get back to court. (*He exits. Wemmick picks up Pip's valise, they stroll.*)
WEMMICK. So, you've never been to London? I was new here, once, myself. But now I know the moves of it.
PIP. Is it a very wicked place?
WEMMICK. You may get cheated, robbed and murdered in London. But there are plenty of people anywhere who'll do that for you. Here we are, "Mr. Pocket, Jr." (*He knocks.*) As I keep the cash, we shall likely be meeting often. (*They shake hands, Wemmick goes.*)

Barnard's Inn.
Herbert comes to the door.

HERBERT. Mr. Pip?
PIP. Mr. Pocket? (*They shake hands.*)
HERBERT. Pray, come in. We're rather bare here, but I hope you'll make out tolerably well.
PIP. It seems very grand to me.
HERBERT. Look around. It's not splendid, because I don't earn very much at present, still I think . . . bless me, you're — you're the prowling boy in Miss Havisham's garden!
PIP. And you are the pale young gentleman!
HERBERT. The idea of its being you!
PIP. The idea of its being you! (*They laugh, both strike a boxing pose.*)
HERBERT. I do hope you've forgiven me for having knocked you about? (*They laugh, shake hands again.*)
NARRATION. Dinner was sent up from the coffee-house in the next road and the young men sat down to get acquainted.
PIP. Mr. Pocket, I was brought up to be a blacksmith. I know little of polite manners. I'd take it as a kindness if you'd give me a hint whenever I go wrong.
HERBERT. With pleasure. And will you do me the kindness of calling me by my Christian name: Herbert?
PIP. With pleasure. My name is Philip.
HERBERT. Philip. Philip . . . no, I don't take to it. Sounds like a highly moral boy in a schoolbook. I know! We're so har-

monious — and you have been a blacksmith . . . would you mind if I called you "Handel"?
PIP. Handel? Why?
HERBERT. There's a piece of music I like, The Harmonious Blacksmith, by Handel — (*He hums the tune.*)
PIP. I'd like it very much. So . . . we two go way back to Miss Havisham's garden! (*They eat.*)
HERBERT. Yes. She's a tartar, isn't she?
PIP. Miss Havisham?
HERBERT. I don't say no to that, but I meant Estella. You know the old lady raised her to wreak revenge on all the male sex?
PIP. No! Revenge for what?
HERBERT. Dear me, it's quite a story — which I'll begin, Handel, by mentioning that in London it's not the custom to put the knife in the mouth — scarcely worth mentioning, but. . . . Also, the spoon is not generally used overhand, but under. This has two advantages: you get to your mouth more easily, but to your cravat less well. Now, as to Miss H. Her father was a country gentleman. There were two children, she and a half-brother named Arthur. Arthur grew up extravagant, undutiful — in a word, bad! So the father disinherited him — Have another glass of wine, and excuse my mentioning that society as a body does not expect one to be so strictly consciencious in emptying one's glass as to turn it upside-down.
PIP. So sorry.
HERBERT. It's nothing. Upon her father's death, Miss H. became an heiress. She was considered a great match. There now appears on the scene — at the races, say, or at a ball — a man who courted the heiress. This is twenty-five years ago, remember. Also remember that your dinner napkin need not be stuffed into your glass. At any rate, her suitor professed love and devotion, and she fell passionately in love. She gave the man huge sums of money, against all advice — particularly against my father's; which is why she's never liked us since, and why I wasn't the boy chosen to come play with Estella — Where was I? Oh yes, the marriage-day was fixed, the wedding-dress bought, the guests invited, the bride-cake baked. The great day arrived — but the bridegroom failed to. Instead, he sent his regrets. That morning a letter arrived —

PIP. Which she received while she was dressing for her wedding? At exactly twenty minutes to nine?
HERBERT. Which is why she had all the clocks in the place stopped at that moment! It was later discovered that the man she loved had conspired with her brother to defraud her. They shared the profits of her sorrow.
PIP. Whatever became of them?
HERBERT. Fell into ruin and disappeared, both of 'em. Not many months after, Miss H. adopted Estella—she was a tiny child. And now, my dear Handel, you know everything I do about poor Miss H.
PIP. But I know nothing of you. If it's not rude to ask, what do you do for a living?
HERBERT. (*Dreamily.*) I'd like to go into business. I'd like to be an insurer of great ships that sail to distant ports.
PIP. I see.
HERBERT. I'm also considering the mining business . . . Africa.
PIP. I see.
HERBERT. Trading in the East Indies interests me.
PIP. I see. You'll need a lot of capital for all that.
HERBERT. True. Meanwhile, I'm looking about me. Temporarily employed in a counting house, but looking about me for the right opportunity. . . .
PIP. And then . . . what larks.
HERBERT. Pardon? (*Pip laughs, Herbert joins him.*)

NARRATION.
Pip took up his studies with Herbert's father, Mr. Matthew Pocket.

He was joined in his classes by another student, a haughty young man named—
DRUMMLE. —Bentley Drummle, seventh in line for a small baronetcy. And who, may I ask, are you?
NARRATION.
Latin, French, history, mathematics in the mornings.

In the afternoons sports, of which the favorite was
rowing on the river.
DRUMMLE. No, no, no, Mr. Pip. Starboard's there. This is port!
PIP. Thank you very much.
DRUMMLE. Now you dip the *blade* of the oar into the water—that's the wide part, Mr. Pip.
PIP. You're too kind. But I did grow up near the river.
DRUMMLE. Yes, I've heard about you. Your rowing lacks form, there's no style to it, is there? Still, you're strong. One might say you've got the arm of a blacksmith! (*Pip glares at him.*)
NARRATION.
To his surprise, Pip enjoyed his studies with Mr. Pocket.

He also enjoyed his tailor, his linendraper, his glovemaker, his jeweler—

Jagger's Office.
Jaggers washes his hands. Wemmick watches.

JAGGERS. Well, how much do you need this time?
PIP. I'm not sure, Mr. Jaggers.
JAGGERS. Fifty pounds?
PIP. Oh, not that much, sir.
JAGGERS. Five pounds?
PIP. Well, more than that, perhaps.
JAGGERS. Twice five? Three times five? Wemmick, twenty pounds for Mr. Pip.
WEMMICK. Twenty pounds in portable property, yes, sir.
JAGGERS. And now excuse me, young man, I'm late to court. (*He goes. Pip stares after him.*)
PIP. I don't know what to make of that man!
WEMMICK. He don't mean you to know, either. He always acts like he's just baited a trap. He sits watching, and suddenly—snap! You're caught. By the way, if you've nothing better to do at the moment, perhaps you'd like to come home with me for supper. I live down in Walworth.
PIP. Why, that's very kind of you. Yes.

WEMMICK. You've no objection to an Aged Parent?
PIP. Certainly not. (*They stroll.*)
WEMMICK. Because I have one.
PIP. I look forward to meeting her—
WEMMICK. Him. Have you been to dine at Mr. Jagger's yet?
PIP. Not yet.
WEMMICK. He'll give you an excellent meal. While you're there, do notice his housekeeper.
PIP. Shall I see something uncommon?
WEMMICK. You will see a wild beast tamed.

Walworth. The garden, with drawbridge.

NARRATION. And so they arrived at Mr. Wemmick's cottage in Walworth. The place was odd, to say the least.
WEMMICK. Step over the drawbridge, if you will, Mr. Pip. (*Pip crosses over with Wemmick, who has grown very affable.*) I must warn you, our little cannon fires at nine o'clock every evening, Greenwich time, so you won't be alarmed.
PIP. It's wonderfully . . . original here. (*The Aged Parent enters, pulling a small cannon on wheels.*)
WEMMICK. Ah, here's the Aged. (*Very loud.*) Well, Aged Parent, how are you this evening?
AGED PARENT. All right, John, all right.
WEMMICK. Here's Mr. Pip, come to tea. (*To Pip.*) Nod at him, Mr. Pip, that's what he likes. He's deaf as a post, he is. (*Pip nods at the Aged, who nods back.*)
AGED PARENT. This is a fine place my son's got, sir. (*Pip nods. Aged nods.*)
WEMMICK. Proud as punch, ain't you, Aged? (*All three nod.*) There's a nod for you, and there's another for you. (*To Pip.*) Mr. Jaggers knows nothing of all this. Never even heard of the Aged. I'll be grateful if you don't mention it— the office is one thing, private life's another. I speak now in my Walworth capacity.
PIP. Not a word, upon my honor.
WEMMICK. When I go to the office I leave the castle behind me, and vice versa. One minute to nine—gun-fire time. It's the Aged Parent's treat. Ready? Here we go! (*There is a big boom.*)

AGED. It's fired! I heard it! (*All three nod happily.*)
NARRATION. A few weeks later, Pip was invited, along with Herbert and Bentley Drummle, to dine at Mr. Jagger's.

Jaggers' Home. A dining table.

JAGGERS. (*Aside, to Pip.*) I like your friend Drummle, he reminds me of a spider.
PIP. He's not my friend, we merely study together. He's a poor scholar, and he is incredibly rude.
JAGGERS. Good. You keep clear of him, he's trouble. But I like such fellows. Yes, he's a real spider. (*Molly appears. Jaggers turns to her.*) Molly, Molly, Molly, Molly, may we sit down? (*She nods. He turns to the others.*) Ah, dinner is served, gentlemen. (*They sit, she serves.*)
NARRATION.
Pip studied her carefully. The night before, he had
been to the theatre to see "Macbeth." The woman's
face resembled those he had seen rise out of the
witches' cauldron. She was humble and silent . . .
but there was something about her. . . .
JAGGERS. So, Mr. Drummle, in addition to conjugating the past conditional tense of French verbs, you gentlemen also go rowing for exercise?
DRUMMLE. We do. And your Mr. Pip's rowing is better than his French—
HERBERT. —I say, Drummle!
DRUMMLE. But I'm stronger with an oar than either of these fellows.
JAGGERS. Really? You talk of strength? I'll show you strength Molly, show them your wrists.
MOLLY. (*Cringes.*) Master, don't—
JAGGERS. Show them, Molly! (*He grabs her arm, runs his finger up and down her wrist delicately.*) There's power, here. Few men have the sinews Molly has, see? Remarkable force, beautiful power. Beautiful. That'll do, Molly, you've been admired, now you may go. (*She goes.*) To your health, gentlemen. (*Darkness.*)

BIDDY. My dear Mr. Pip: I write at the request of Mr. Gargery, for to let you know he is coming up to London and would be glad to see you. He will call at Barnard's Hotel next Tuesday morning at nine. Your sister continues to linger. Your ever obedient servant, Biddy. P.S. He wishes me most particular to write "what larks!" He says you will understand. I hope you will see him, even though you *are* a gentleman now, for you had ever a good heart and he is so worthy. He asks me again to write "what larks!" Biddy.
NARRATION.
With what feelings did Pip look forward to Joe's visit?

With pleasure? No, with considerable disturbance and mortification.

What would Bentley Drummle think of someone like Joe?

And what would Joe think of Pip's expensive and rather aimless new life?

Barnard's Inn.
A knock at the door. Joe enters, awkwardly dressed in a suit.

PIP. Joe! (*Joe holds his arms out to embrace Pip, Pip sticks out his right hand. They shake.*)
JOE. Pip, old chap.
PIP. I'm glad to see you, Joe. Come in, give me your hat! (*Joe remembers he has one, removes it from his head, but holds fast to it.*)
JOE. Which you have that grow'd and that swelled with the gentlefolk!
PIP. And you look wonderfully well, Joe. Shall I take your hat? (*Joe continues to clutch it.*)
JOE. Your poor sister's no worse nor no better than she was. And Biddy is ever right and ready, that girl. (*Herbert enters from bedroom.*)
PIP. Here's my friend, Herbert Pocket. Joe. (*Herbert extends his hand, Joe drops his hat.*)
HERBERT. Your servant, sir.
JOE. Yours, yours. (*He picks up the hat.*)
HERBERT. Well. Have you seen anything of London, yet?
JOE. Why, yes, sir. Soon as I left the coach, I went straight off

to look at the Blacking Factory warehouse.
HERBERT. Really? What did you think?
JOE. It don't come near to its likeness on the labels.
HERBERT. Is that so?
JOE. See, on the labels it is drawn too architectooralooral. (*Herbert nods. Pip covers his face in mortification. Joe drops his hat.*)
HERBERT. You're quite right about that, Mr. Gargery—he is, Pip. Well, I must be off to work. It's good to have met you. (*He offers his hand. Joe reaches, drops his hat. Herbert goes out.*)
JOE. We two being alone, sir—
PIP. —Joe, how can you call me "sir?!"
JOE. Us two being alone, Pip, and me having the intention to stay not many minutes more—
PIP. —Joe!—
JOE. I will now conclude—leastways begin—what led up to my having the present honor, sir. Miss Havisham has a message for you, Pip, sir. She says to tell you Miss Estella has come home from abroad and will be happy to see you.
PIP. Estella!
JOE. I tried to get Biddy to write the message to you, sir, but she says, "I know Pip will be glad to have that message by word of mouth." Which I have now concluded. (*He starts to go.*) And so, Pip, I wish you ever well and ever prospering to greater height, sir—
PIP. —You're not leaving?!
JOE. Which I am.
PIP. But surely you're coming back for dinner?
JOE. Pip, old chap, life is made of ever-so-many partings welded together, and one man's a blacksmith, and one's a whitesmith, and one's a goldsmith. Diwisions among such must be met as they come. You and me is not two figures to be seen together in London. I'm wrong in these clothes. I'm wrong out of the forge. You won't find half so much fault in me if you think of me in my forge clothes, with my hammer in my hand. And so, ever the best of friends, Pip. God bless you, dear old chap, God bless you, sir.
NARRATION.
And he was gone.

After the first guilty flow of repentence, Pip thought
better of such feelings.

He dried his eyes, and did not follow Joe into the street to bring him back.

The next day Pip took the coach down from London.

He did not bother to call in at the forge.

Miss Havisham's.
Estella waits in the shadows. Pip enters.

HAVISHAM. So, you kiss my hand as if I were a queen?
PIP. I heard you wished to see me, so I came directly.
HAVISHAM. Well? (*Estella turns, smiles at him.*) Do you find her much changed?
PIP. I . . .
HAVISHAM. And is he changed, Estella?
ESTELLA. Very much.
HAVISHAM. Less coarse and common? (*Estella laughs.*) Go into the garden, you two, and give me some peace until tea time. (*Estella takes his arm, they wander out.*)
PIP. Look it's all still here.
ESTELLA. I must have been a singular little creature. I hid over there and watched you fight that strange boy. I enjoyed that battle very much.
PIP. You rewarded me very much.
ESTELLA. Did I? (*She picks up a clay pot of primroses, smells them, picks one and puts it in Pip's buttonhole.*)
PIP. He and I are great friends, now. It was there you made me cry, that first day.
ESTELLA. Did I? I don't remember. (*She notices his hurt.*) You must understand, I have no heart. That may have something to do with my poor memory.
PIP. I know better, Estella.
ESTELLA. Oh, I've a heart to be stabbed in or shot at, no doubt. But I've no softness there, no . . . sympathy. If we're to be thrown together often—and it seems we shall be—you'd better believe that of me. What's wrong, is Pip scared? Will he cry? Come, come, tea's ready. You shall not shed tears for my cruelty today. Give me your arm, I must deliver you safely back to

Miss Havisham. (*They return to Miss Havisham, who takes Estella's hand and kisses it with ravenous intensity. Estella goes out.*)
HAVISHAM. Is she not beautiful, Pip? Graceful? Do you admire her?
PIP. Everyone who sees her must.
HAVISHAM. Love her, love her, love her! If she favors you, love her! If she wounds you, love her! If she tears your heart to pieces, love her, love her, love her!
PIP. You make that word sound like a curse.
HAVISHAM. You know what love is? I do. It is blind devotion, unquestioning self-humiliation, utter submission. It is giving up your whole heart and soul to the one who smites you, as I did. That is love. (*Darkness.*)
NARRATION.
Love her!

Love her!

Love her!

The words rang triumphantly in his ears all the way back to London.

That Estella was destined for him, once a blacksmith's boy!

And if she were not yet rapturously grateful for that destiny,

He would somehow awaken her sleeping heart!

Barnard's Inn.

PIP. I've got something particular to tell you.
HERBERT. That's odd, I've something to tell you.
PIP. It concerns myself—and one other person.
HERBERT. That's odd, too.
PIP. Herbert, I love—I adore Estella!
HERBERT. Oh, I know that. My dear Handel, you brought your adoration along with your valise the day you came to London.

PIP. She's come home—I saw her yesterday. I do love her so!
HERBERT. What are the young lady's sentiments?
PIP. Alas, she is miles and miles away from me.
HERBERT. If that's so, can you not detach yourself from her? (*Pip turns away.*) Think of her upbringing—think of Miss Havisham! Given all that, your love could lead to misery.
PIP. I know, but I cannot help myself. I cannot "detach."
HERBERT. Well. But perhaps it doesn't matter—perhaps your feelings are justified. After all, it would seem you've been chosen for her. Yes, I'm sure it will work out!
PIP. What a hopeful disposition you have.
HERBERT. I must have—I've not got much else. But since the subject's come up, I want you to know first—I'm engaged.
PIP. My dear Herbert! May I ask the bride's name?
HERBERT. Name of Clara. Clara Barley.
PIP. And does Clara Barley live in London?
HERBERT. She does. Oh Pip, if you could see her—so lovely!
PIP. Is she rich?
HERBERT. Poorer than me—and as sweet as she is poor. I'm going to marry her—
PIP. That's wonderful, Herbert. When? (*Herbert's face falls.*)
HERBERT. That's the trouble. A fellow can't marry while he's still looking about him, can he?
PIP. I don't suppose he can. But cheer up, it will all work out. Yes, I feel it . . . it *shall* work out!

ESTELLA. Dear Pip: I am coming to London the day after tomorrow, by midday coach. Miss Havisham insists that you are to meet me, and I write in obedience to her wishes. Yours, Estella.
NARRATION. And suddenly she was there, in London! (*Estella hands a valise and hatbox to Pip.*)
PIP. I'm glad, so glad you've come.
ESTELLA. Yes. I'm to live here with a chaperone, at great—ridiculous expense, really. She is to take me about. She's to show people to me, and show me to people.
PIP. I wonder Miss Havisham could part with you.
ESTELLA. It's all part of her great plan. She wants me to write her constantly and report how I get on—

PIP. Get on? Get on? With what? With whom? (*Estella smiles.*)
ESTELLA. Poor Pip. Dear Pip.

BIDDY. Dear Pip: I am writing to inform you that your sister died at peace the night before last. Her funeral was held this morning. We discussed whether to wait until you could attend it, but decided that as you are busy in your life as a gentleman we should go forward with the affair as we are. Yours, Biddy.
P.S. Joe sends his fond wishes and sympathy.
NARRATION.
As Pip got on, he became accustomed to the idea of his great expectations.

He grew careless with his money, contracting a great quantity of debts.

And Herbert's good nature combined with Pip's lavish spending, to lead them both into habits they could ill-afford.

They moved their lodgings from the spartan Barnard's Inn to more luxurious quarters in the Temple, on the banks of the Thames.
   (*Herbert and Pip enter, each holding sheaves of bills.*)
PIP. My dear Herbert, we are getting on very badly.
HERBERT. My dear Handel, those very words were on my lips! We must reform.
PIP. We must indeed. (*They look at each other, toss the bills up in the air, watch them float down.*)
NARRATION.
Their affairs went from bad to worse, so they began to look forward eagerly to Pip's twenty-first birthday—

—In the hope that Mr. Jaggers, by way of celebration, might give Pip some concrete evidence of his expectations.

Jagger's Office.
Jaggers is washing his hands.

WEMMICK. Happy birthday, Mr. Pip. (*To Jaggers.*) He's here.

JAGGERS. Well, well, twenty-one today, is that not the case?
PIP. Guilty, sir. I confess to being twenty-one.
JAGGERS. Tell me, Pip, what are you living at the rate of?
PIP. I . . . don't know, sir.
JAGGERS. I thought as much. Now it's your turn to ask me a question.
PIP. Have—have I anything to receive today?
JAGGERS. I thought we'd come to that! Take this piece of paper in your hand. Now unfold it. What is it?
PIP. It's a banknote . . . for five hundred pounds!
JAGGERS. And a handsome sum of money, too, you agree?
PIP. How could I do otherwise?
JAGGERS. It is yours. And at the rate of five hundred per year, *and no more,* you are to live until your benefactor chooses to appear.
PIP. Is my benefactor to be made known to me today?
JAGGERS. As to *when* that person decides to be identified, why, that's nothing to do with me, I'm only the agent—
PIP. But she—
JAGGERS. —She?—
PIP. —My patron—
JAGGERS. —Hah! You cannot trick me into giving evidence, young man. Now, excuse me, I'm off to court. (*He goes, followed by Wemmick. Pip stares at the banknote, holds it up, suddenly starts to smile.*)
NARRATION.
The following Sunday Pip made a pilgrimage down to Walworth to see Mr. Wemmick.

For he had an idea about how he would like to spend at least part of his money.

> *Walworth.*
> *Pip crosses over the little drawbridge.*
> *The Aged Parent greets him.*

AGED PARENT. Ah, my son will be home at any moment, young man. (*Pip nods.*) Make yourself at home. You made acquaintance with my son at his office? (*Pip nods.*) I hear he's a wonderful hand at his business. (*Pip nods.*) Now to be precise, I don't actually *hear* it, mind, for I'm hard of hearing.

PIP. Not really!

AGED PARENT. Oh, but I am! Look, here comes John, and Miss Skiffins with him. All right, John?

WEMMICK. All right, Aged P. So sorry I wasn't here to greet you, Mr. Pip. May I present Miss Skiffins, who is a friend of mine, and a neighbor. The Aged and Miss Skiffins will prepare tea, while we chat —

PIP. I wish to ask you — you are in your Walworth frame of mind, I presume? (*Wemmick nods, the Aged nods, they all nod.*)

WEMMICK. I am. I shall speak in a private and personal capacity. (*Miss Skiffins leads the Aged away.*)

PIP. I wish to do something for my friend, Herbert Pocket. He has been the soul of kindness and I've ill-repaid him by encouraging him to spend more than he has. He'd have been better off if I'd never come along, poor fellow, but as I have, I want to help him. Tell me, how can I set him up in a small partnership somewhere?

WEMMICK. That's devilish good of you, Mr. Pip.

PIP. Only he must never know I had any part in it. You know the extent of my resources, Wemmick. Can you help me? (*Wemmick thinks for a moment.*)

WEMMICK. Perhaps . . . perhaps — yes! Yes, I like it. But it must be done by degrees. We'll go to work on it! (*Miss Skiffins appears.*)

SKIFFINS. Mr. Wemmick, dear, the Aged is toasting.

PIP. I beg your pardon, but what did she say?

WEMMICK. Tea is served. (*They go off.*)

NARRATION.
Before a week had passed, Wemmick found a worthy young shipping broker named Clarriker —

Who wanted intelligent help —

And who also wanted some capital —

And who might eventually want a partner.

Between this young merchant and Pip secret papers were
signed, and half of Pip's five hundred pounds disappeared.

The whole business was so cleverly managed that Herbert
hadn't the least suspicion that Pip's hand was in it.
    (*Herbert races in to find Pip reading.*)
HERBERT. Handel, Handel, I've the most mighty piece of
news! I've just come from an interview in the City — man name
of Clarriker — I'm to have a position there and — oh, Handel, I
start next week, and I might, in time —
PIP. I'm happy for you, Herbert, so happy —
NARRATION.
Pip went quickly into his room and wept with joy
at the thought that his expectations had at last
done some good to somebody.

But what of Estella?

She rapidly became the belle of London, seen and
admired by all.

Pip never had an hour's happiness in her society —

Yet his mind, twenty-four hours a day, harped on
the happiness of possessing her someday.

On the occasion of Miss Havisham's birthday they were
asked to come down from London together to visit.

    Miss Havisham's.
    Pip bows. Estella kisses her cheek. Miss Havisham clutches
    Estella's hand.

HAVISHAM. How does she use you, Pip, how does she use
you?
PIP. According to your designs, I fear.
NARRATION.
And he suddenly saw his fate . . .

In the cobwebs . . .

In the decayed wedding cake . . .

In the face of the clocks that had stopped . . .

And his profound sadness communicated itself to Estella.
 (*Estella withdraws her hand from Miss Havisham.*)
HAVISHAM. What, are you tired of me?
ESTELLA. Only a little tired of myself.
HAVISHAM. No, speak the truth, you're tired of me! (*Estella shivers, turns away.*) You cold, cold heart.
ESTELLA. What? You reproach me for being cold? I am what you made me—take all the credit or blame.
HAVISHAM. Look at her, so thankless. I took you to my heart when it was still bleeding from its wounds.
ESTELLA. Yes, yes, what would you have of me?
HAVISHAM. Love.
ESTELLA. Mother-by-adoption, how can I return to you what you never gave me?
HAVISHAM. Did I never give her love? You are so proud, so proud!
ESTELLA. Who taught me to be proud? Who praised me when I learned my lesson?
HAVISHAM. So hard, so hard!
ESTELLA. Who taught me to be hard?—
HAVISHAM. But to be proud and hard to me—to *me,* Estella!
ESTELLA. I cannot think what makes you so unreasonable, when Pip and I have ridden all the way down here for your birthday. I have never forgotten the wrongs done you. I've learned the lessons you taught me—God knows I wish I could unlearn them! (*Pause. Estella comes to her, kisses her.*)
NARRATION. And as soon as the quarrel began, it was over, and never referred to again. (*Estella leads Miss Havisham off.*)

NARRATION. The following week, Herbert and Pip were dining at their club.
DRUMMLE. Gentlemen, raise your glasses. I give you Estella.
PIP. Estella who?
DRUMMLE. Estella of Havisham, a peerless beauty.
HERBERT. (*To Pip.*) Much he knows of beauty, the idiot.

PIP. I am acquainted with that lady you speak of. Why do you propose a toast to one of whom you know nothing?
DRUMMLE. Ah, but I do not know her. I escorted her to the opera last night.
NARRATION.
Now she was seen around the town with Drummle,

At the theatre, at a ball, at the races . . .

But wasn't she destined for Pip?

He took comfort in that thought, and in Herbert's happiness —

For *he* had Clara Barley.

And so, two years passed.

The Temple Apartment.
Night. Pip sits reading.

NARRATION.
It was the night of Pip's twenty-third birthday.

The weather was wretched, wet and stormy.

St. Paul's had just chimed eleven when —

Pip thought he heard a footstep on the stair.
PIP. Who's there? (*He puts down his book, takes up a candle.*) Answer! There's someone down there, is there not?
MAGWITCH. (*In shadows.*) Yes.
PIP. What floor do you want?
MAGWITCH. The top. Mr. Pip.
PIP. That is my name. Pray, state your business. (*Magwitch slowly emerges from the shadows, warmly dressed in seafaring clothes. He holds out his hands to Pip.*)
MAGWITCH. My business?
PIP. Who are you? Explain, please. (*Magwitch advances.*) I don't understand — keep away — !
MAGWITCH. It's disappointing to a man, arter having looked for'ard so distant and come so far, but you're not to blame for that. (*He gazes at Pip admiringly.*) You're a game 'un. I'm glad

you grow'd up a game 'un. (*He takes off his cap. Pip freezes.*) You acted nobly out on that marsh, my dear boy, and I never forgot it! And now I've come back to you! I've come back to you, Pip, dear boy! (*And to Pip's horror, Magwitch throws his arms around him and embraces him. Darkness.*)

END ACT ONE

ACT TWO

The Temple.
As it was at the end of Act One. Magwitch embraces the horrified Pip.

MAGWITCH. I've come back to you, Pip, dear boy!
PIP. I know you now, and if you're grateful for what I did on those marshes years ago, that's fine, but—
MAGWITCH. You look to have done well since then.
PIP. I have—please release me, I beg you. (*Magwitch lets go of Pip.*)
MAGWITCH. May I make so bold as to ask *how* you have done well since you and me was out on those shiverin' marshes?
PIP. How? I've been chosen to succeed to some property.
MAGWITCH. Might a warmint ask *what* property?
PIP. (*Brief pause.*) I don't know.
MAGWITCH. Might a warmint ask *whose* property?
PIP. (*A long pause.*) I . . . don't know. . . .
MAGWITCH. Might there be some kind of guardian in the picture, then; some lawyer, maybe? And the first letter of this lawyer's name, could it be . . . J? For Jaggers?!
PIP. My God—no! No, it can't be . . . you!
MAGWITCH. Yes, Pip, dear boy, I've made a gentleman on you—it's me wot done it! I'm your second father, lad, and I've come back to you, to see my fine gentleman—(*He embraces Pip again.*) Didn't you never think it could be me? (*Pip disengages with a wail.*)
PIP. Never! Never, never, never!
HERBERT. (*Entering in his dressing gown.*) I say, Handel, you're making an awful racket—oh, I beg your pardon, I didn't know you had company. . . . (*Magwitch takes a knife out.*)
PIP. Herbert, this is . . . a visitor of mine. (*Pip sees the knife. To Magwitch:*) He's got every right to be here—he *lives* here! He is my friend.
MAGWITCH. (*Puts away knife, takes out little Bible.*) Then it's all right, dear boy. Take the book in your hand, Pip's friend. Lord strike you dead it you ever split in any way sumever. Kiss the book. (*Herbert does so.*)

PIP. Herbert, this is my . . . benefactor. (*Herbert gapes.*)
HERBERT. Oh . . . I . . . how do you do, my name's Herbert Pocket. I hope you're quite well . . . ?
MAGWITCH. How do you do, Pip's companion. And never believe me if Pip shan't make a gentleman on you, too!
HERBERT. I'll look forward to it. Ah . . . Pip? (*Pip shrugs at him, bewildered.*)
PIP. Tell me, do you have a name? By what do I call you?
MAGWITCH. Name of Magwitch. Christened Abel.
HERBERT. Abel Magwitch, fancy . . .
MAGWITCH. I were born and raised to be a warmint, but now I'm Pip's second father, and he's my son. More to me than any son. Every since I was transported to Australia, I swore that each time I earned a guinea, that guinea should go to Pip. And I swore that when I speculated and got rich, it'd all be for Pip. I lived rough so that he should live smooth. (*He admires Pip benevolently.*) How good-looking he have grow'd. There's a pair of bright eyes somewheres wot you love, eh, Pip? Those eyes shall be yourn, dear boy, if money can buy 'em. (*He beams at Pip, yawns.*) Now then, where shall I sleep tonight?
PIP. Pray, take my bedroom.
MAGWITCH. By your leave, I'll latch the door first. Caution is necessary. (*He does so.*)
HERBERT. Caution? How do you mean, caution?
MAGWITCH. (*Whispers.*) It's death.
HERBERT. (*Whispers.*) What's death?
MAGWITCH. If I'm caught. I was sent up for life, warn't I? It's death for me to come back to England; I'd be hang'd for it, if I was took.
PIP. (*An anguished explosion.*) Then why in God's name have you come?!!
MAGWITCH. To see my dear boy. To watch him be a fine gentleman. (*He nods, beams, exits into the bedroom. Pip buries his head in his hands.*)
PIP. Estella, Estella . . . I am lost!
HERBERT. Hold steady — he mustn't hear you.
PIP. The shame of it, Herbert! I always thought Miss Havisham — I thought Estella was intended for me. Fool. Foolish dreamer! And now I awaken to find I owe my fortune to this man, this wretched . . . criminal! . . . who has risked his life to

51

be with me! It's a terrible joke, isn't it? And you know what's the funniest part? I scorned my most faithful friend for these "expectations!" Joe, Joe. . . .
HERBERT. Take hold of yourself, Handel. There are practical questions to answer. How are we to keep him out of danger? Where will he live? (*Dreamily.*) There are disguises, I suppose . . . wigs, spectacles. Given his intimidating manner, we can hardly dress him up as a vicar but. . . . I think some sort of prosperous farmer's disguise would be best. We shall cut his hair! (*He looks at the suffering Pip.*) Get some sleep, Handel. You'll need it when morning comes.
PIP. When morning comes, Mr. Jaggers had better have a good explanation!

Mr. Jagger's Office.

NARRATION.
The moment Pip walked in, Mr. Jaggers could see from his face that the man had turned up.

Jaggers immediately immersed himself in soap and water.
JAGGERS. Now Pip, be careful! Don't *tell* me anything—I don't want to be told a thing! I am not curious.
PIP. I merely wish to be sure that what *I've* been told is true.
JAGGERS. Did you say *told* or *informed?* Told would imply verbal communication, face-to-face. You cannot have verbal communication with a man who's still in Australia, can you?
PIP. Lawyers' games!
JAGGERS. Games? The difference between the two verbs could mean a man's safety—his life!
PIP. I shall say "informed," Mr. Jaggers.
JAGGERS. Good.
PIP. I have been informed by a man named Abel Magwitch that he is my benefactor.
JAGGERS. That is the man. In New South Wales, Australia.
PIP. And only he?
JAGGERS. Only he.
PIP. I don't wish to make you responsible for my mistaken conclusions, but I always supposed it was Miss Havisham.

JAGGERS. As you say, Pip, that's not my fault. Not a particle of evidence to support that conclusion. (*Pip leaves.*) Never judge by appearances—irrefutable evidence, that's the rule. Evidence!

The Temple.

NARRATION.
During the following days, Pip studied Magwitch as he napped in the chair,

Wondering what evils the man had committed,

Loading him with all the crimes in the calendar!
(*As Magwitch dozes in the chair, Pip studies him. Herbert enters, lays a sympathetic hand on Pip's shoulder.*)
HERBERT. Dear Pip, what's to be done?
PIP. I'm too stunned to think. I could run away for a soldier.
HERBERT. Of course you can't. He's strongly attached to you.
PIP. He disgusts me—his look, his manners!
HERBERT. But you've got to get him out of England, to safety. And you'll have to go with him or else he won't leave.
PIP. You're right, of course. He's risked his life on my account; it's up to me to keep him from throwing it away altogether.
HERBERT. Well said! We'll see the matter through together—
(*Pip seizes his hand in gratitude. Magwitch wakes up, smiles.*)
MAGWITCH. Ah, dear boy, and Pip's companion: I was napping.
PIP. Magwitch, I must ask you something. Do you remember that day long ago, on the marshes?
MAGWITCH. I do, dear boy.
PIP. You were fighting with another convict when the soldiers caught you—you recall?
MAGWITCH. I should think so! What of it?
HERBERT. If we're to help you, we must know more about that day . . . and about you.
MAGWITCH. You're still on your oath?
HERBERT. Assuredly.
MAGWITCH. (*He takes out his pipe, the young men sit.*) Dear boy, and Pip's companion, I could tell you my life short and

handy, if you like: in-jail and out-of-jail, in-jail and out-of-jail. I know'd my name to be Magwitch, christened Abel—but I've no notion of where I was born, or to who. I first came aware of myself down in Essex, stealing turnips for my food. Thereafter there warn't a soul that seed young Abel Magwitch but wot took fright at him and drove him off. Or turned him in. I can see me, a pitiable ragged little creetur, who eveyone called "hardened." "This boy's a terrible hardened one." "This one spends his life in prisons." Then they'd preach at me about the devil and let me go. But wot the devil's a boy to do with no home and an empty stomach? So I'd steal food again, and be turned in again. Somehow I managed to grow up . . . tramping, begging, thieving . . . a bit of a laborer, a bit of a poacher. And so I got to be a man. One day I was lounging about Epsom races, when I met a man. Him whose skull I'd crack wi' pleasure if I saw him now. His name was Compeyson. And that's the man you saw me a-pounding in the marshes that day long ago.

PIP. Compeyson.

MAGWITCH. Ay. Smooth and good-looking was Compeyson. He had book-learning, so he set hisself up as a gentleman. He found me, as I say, at the races. "To judge from appearances, you're out of luck," he says. "I've never been in it," I answers him. "Luck changes," he says. "What can you do?" "Eat and drink," says I. So Compeyson took me on, to be his man and partner. And what was his business? Swindling, forgery, stolen bank-note passing; suchlike. He had no more heart than an iron file. —There was another man in the game with Compeyson—as was called Arthur. (*Pip and Herbert glance at each other.*) Mister Arthur. Poor fellow was in a sad state of decline. Him and Compeyson had been in some wicked business together—they'd made a pot of money off some rich lady a few years before. (*Herbert and Pip look at each other.*) But Compeyson had gambled it all away long since. Mr. Arthur had the look of a dying man when I first took up wi' them—from which I should have took warning. Soon after I came, Mr. Arthur took very ill and began crying, delirious-like, that he was haunted. "She's coming for me—I can't get rid of her. She's all dressed in white, wi' white flowers in her hair." And Compeyson says to poor Mr. Arthur, "She's alive, you fool. She's living in her wreck of a house in the country." And Mr. Arthur says, "No, she's here, in

her white dress; and over her heart there are drops of blood—
you broke her heart! And now she's coming to hang a shroud on
me!" And so he died. Compeyson took it as good riddance.
Next day him and me started work. I won't tell you what we
did. I'll simply say the man got me into such nets and traps as
made me his slave. He were smarter than me. He used his head
and he used my legs to keep his own self out of trouble. He had
no mercy! My missus—no, wait, I don't meanter bring my
missus in—(*He looks about him, confused.*) No need to go into
that. But Compeyson! When we two was finally caught and put
on trial, I noticed what a gentleman he looked wi' his curly hair
and his pocket handkerchief, and what a common wretch I
looked. Judge and jury thought so too, and even the great Mr.
Jaggers couldn't get me justice that day. For when it's time for
sentencing, it's him wot gets seven years and me wot gets four-
teen! Arter the trial, we was on the same prison ship—I paid
him back—I smashed his face in. You seed the scar, dear boy.
Then I found a way to escape, and I swam to shore, where I
first saw you, in among those old graves.
HERBERT. What an astonishing tale!
MAGWITCH. And true. Little Pip gave me to understand
that Compeyson had escaped too, and was out on them
marshes. And I vowed then and there, whatever the cost to me,
I would drag that scoundrel back to the prison ship. And I did,
too. I did.
PIP. Is Compeyson dead?
MAGWITCH. He hopes I am, if he's still alive. Well, I've
talked myself near to death. Good night, dear boy. Good night,
Pip's companion. (*He exits into the bedroom. Pause.*)
HERBERT. Handel?
PIP. Yes, I know. Miss Havisham's brother was named Arthur.
HERBERT. Compeyson is the man who broke her heart.
PIP. Herbert, before I get Magwitch out of the country, I must
try to speak with Estella. I must see her once more.

NARRATION.
Pip set off by the early morning coach, and was into
open country when the day came creeping on.

The fields were hung about with mists.

At length the coach stopped at the Blue Boar Inn, which was in the neighborhood of Miss Havisham's house.

When Pip alighted, he was amazed to see a familiar figure lounging by the Inn door.
PIP. Bentley Drummle!
DRUMMLE. You've just come down? (*Pip nods.*) Beastly place. Your part of the country, I think?
PIP. I'm told it's very like your Shropshire.
DRUMMLE. Not in the least like it.
PIP. Have you been here long?
DRUMMLE. Long enough to be tired of it.
PIP. Do you stay here long?
DRUMMLE. Can't say. And you?
PIP. Can't say. (*Drummle gives a brief, unpleasant laugh.*) Are you amused, Mr. Drummle?
DRUMMLE. Not very. I'm about to go riding . . . to explore the marshes. Out-of-the-way villages, here, I'm told, Quaint little public houses. Smithies, too. Boy! (*A stable boy appears.*)
BOY. Yes, sir.
DRUMMLE. Is my horse ready?
BOY. Waiting in the yard, sir.
DRUMMLE. The young lady won't ride today, the weather is too foul. And boy—
BOY. Yes, sir?
DRUMMLE. Tell the innkeeper I plan to dine at the young lady's this evening.
BOY. Quite so, sir. (*Drummle goes. The boy turns to Pip.*) May I help you, sir? (*Pip, in a rage, shies his valise at him.*)

Miss Havisham's.
Miss Havisham is in her bath chair. Estella sits a little apart, knitting.

NARRATION.
Pip found the two women seated by the fire.

Their faces were lit by the candles which burned on the wall.

HAVISHAM. And what wind brings you down here, Pip?
PIP. I wished to see Estella, and hearing that some wind had blown her here, I followed.
HAVISHAM. Pray, sit down.
PIP. What I have to say to Estella, Miss Havisham, I shall say before you. It won't displease you to learn that I am as unhappy as you can ever have meant me to be. (*Miss Havisham says nothing. Estella knits.*) I have found out who my patron is. It's not a pleasant discovery. It's not likely to enrich my reputation.
HAVISHAM. Well?
PIP. When you first brought me here, when I still belonged to that village yonder that I wish I had never left, I suppose I was picked at random, as a kind of servant, to gratify a whim of yours?
HAVISHAM. Ay, Pip.
PIP. And Mr. Jaggers—
HAVISHAM. —Mr. Jaggers had nothing to do with it. His being my lawyer and the lawyer of your patron is coincidence.
PIP. Then why did you lead me on? Was that kind?
HAVISHAM. (*Striking her stick upon the ground.*) Who am I, for God's sake, that I should be kind?!
PIP. In encouraging my mistaken notion, you were also punishing some of your greedy relations?
HAVISHAM. Perhaps.
PIP. There is one branch of that family whom you deeply wrong. I speak of my former tutor, Mr. Matthew Pocket, and his son Herbert. If you think those two to be anything but generous, open and upright, you are in error.
HAVISHAM. You say so because Herbert Pocket is your friend.
PIP. He made himself my friend even when he thought I had taken his place in your affections.
HAVISHAM. Yes, well?
PIP. Miss Havisham, I speak frankly: if you could spare the money to do Herbert a lasting service in life—secretly—I could show you how.
HAVISHAM. Why secretly?
PIP. Because I began the service myself, two years ago, secretly, and I don't wish to be betrayed. Why I cannot complete it myself is . . . it is part of another person's secret. (*Havisham*

stares into the fire. Estella knits.)
HAVISHAM. Well, well, well, what else have you to say?
PIP. Estella, you know I've loved you long and dearly. I'd have spoken sooner, but for my foolish hope that Miss Havisham intended us for one another. Whilst I believed you had no choice in the matter I refrained from speaking, but now . . . (*Estella shakes her head, knits on.*) I know, I know. I've no hope that I shall ever call you mine. (*Again, Estella shakes her head. She knits.*) If she'd have thought about it, she'd have seen how cruel it was to torture me with so vain a hope, but she couldn't see. Poor Miss Havisham: enveloped in her own pain, she could not feel mine. (*Havisham clutches her heart.*)
ESTELLA. It seems there are fancies . . . sentiments—I don't know what to call them—which I cannot comprehend. When you say you love me, I hear your words but they touch nothing here. I did try to warn you.
PIP. Yes.
ESTELLA. But you wouldn't be warned. I am more honest with you than with other men—I can do no more than that.
PIP. Bentley Drummle is here, pursuing you? (*She nods.*) Is it true you encourage him? Ride with him? —Is it true he dines with you today?
ESTELLA. Quite true.
PIP. You cannot love him.
ESTELLA. What have I just told you? I cannot love!
PIP. You would never marry him?
ESTELLA. (*Pause.*) I am going to be married to him.
PIP. Dearest Estella, don't let Miss Havisham lead you into so fatal a step. Forget me—you've already done so, I know—but for the love of God, bestow yourself on a man worthier than Bentley Drummle!
ESTELLA. Wedding preparations have already begun. It is my own act, not hers.
PIP. Your own act, to fling yourself away on a brute?!
ESTELLA. Don't be afraid of my being a blessing to him! (*A pause. Miss Havisham moans.*) As for you, Pip, I trust you'll get me out of your thoughts within a week.
PIP. Out of my thoughts! You have been in every prospect I've seen since I first met you—on the river, in the wind, on the city streets. To the last hour of my life you cannot choose but re-

main part of me. O, God bless you. God forgive you! (*Miss Havisham clutches at her heart again. Pip kisses Estella's hand, leaves.*)
NARRATION.
All done, all gone!

Pip wandered through the lanes and bypaths around the house . . .

Then he turned and walked all the way back to London.

NARRATION.
It was past midnight when he crossed London bridge, closer to one when he approached his lodgings.

He was stopped by the night porter.
PORTER. Urgent message for you, Mr. Pip. (*Pip tears open an envelope, reads, as:*)
WEMMICK. Dear Mr. Pip: Don't go home. Yours, J. Wemmick.
NARRATION.
Pip turned hastily away. He spent the remainder of the night in an hotel in Covent Garden.

Footsore and weary as he was, he could not sleep.

And after an hour, those extraordinary voices with which silence teems began to make themselves audible.

The closet whispered.

The fireplace sighed.

The washstand ticked.

And they all spoke as if with one voice:

Don't go home.

Whatever night-fancies crowded in on him, they never ceased to murmur:

Don't go home.

When at last he dozed in sheer exhaustion, it became

a vast, shadowy verb he had to conjugate, imperative mood, present tense:

Do not thou go home.

Let him or her not go home.

Let us not go home.

Do not ye or you go home.

Early the next morning Pip went to Walworth to consult Wemmick.

This was obviously not a matter for the office.

Walworth.
Pip crosses over the drawbridge.

WEMMICK. You got my note?
PIP. I did.
WEMMICK. I hope you destroyed it. It's never wise to leave documentary evidence if you can help it. (*He hands Pip a sausage speared on a toasting fork.*) Would you mind toasting a sausage for the Aged while we talk?
PIP. Delighted.
WEMMICK. You understand, we're in our private and personal capacities here? (*Pip nods.*) I heard by accident yesterday that a certain person had recently disappeared from Australia, a person possessed of vast portable property. Yes? I also heard that your rooms were being watched, and might be watched again. — All right, ain't you, Aged P? (*He takes the toasting fork from Pip, puts the sausage on a plate for the Aged.*)
AGED PARENT. All right, John, all right, my boy! (*They all nod.*)
PIP. Tell me, the disappearance of this person from Australia and the watching of my rooms — are these two events connected?
WEMMICK. If they aren't yet, they will be. (*They all nod.*)
PIP. Mr. Wemmick, have you ever heard of a man of bad character whose name is Compeyson? (*Wemmick nods.*) Is he

living? (*Wemmick and the Aged nod.*) Is he in London? (*All three nod.*)
WEMMICK. I see you've got the point. When I learned of it, I naturally came to your rooms, and not finding anyone at home — or answering the door, anyway — I went to Clarriker's office to see Mr. Herbert. And without mentioning any names I explained that if he was aware of any Tom, Dick or Richard staying with you, he had better get him out of the way.
PIP. Herbert must have been mystified.
WEMMICK. Not for long. He conceived a plan. Seems he's courting a young lady who lives in Mill Pond Bank, right on the river. And *that's* where Mr. Herbert has lodged this person, this Tom, Dick or Richard! It's a sound idea, because although *you're* being watched, Mr. Herbert isn't . . . And as he visits there often, he can act as go-between!
PIP. Good thinking.
WEMMICK. But there's an even better reason for the move. This house is *by the river.* You understand? (*Pip shakes his head.*) When the right moment comes, you can slip your man aboard a foreign packet-boat unnoticed. Here is the young lady's address in Mill Pond Bank — Miss Barley's the name, and a very odd name it is. You may go there this evening, but do it *before* you go home, so they won't follow you.
PIP. I don't know how to thank you —
WEMMICK. One last piece of advice. You must get hold of your man's portable property as soon as you can. For his sake s well as yours. It mustn't fall into the wrong hands, must it? Well, I'd better be off to the City. I suggest you stay here until dark — you look tired enough. Keep out of sight and spend a restful day with Aged. Ain't that right, Aged P?
AGED PARENT. All right, John.
WEMMICK. Goodbye then, Mr. Pip. (*He goes. Pip stares into the fire.*)
NARRATION.
Pip soon fell asleep before the fire.

He and the Aged Parent enjoyed each other's society by falling asleep before the fire throughout the whole day.

When it was dark, Pip prepared to leave.

The Aged was readying tea, and Pip inferred from the number of cups, three, that a visitor was expected. Could it be that odd lady with the green gloves . . . Miss Skiffins?

Pip made his way to Mill Pond Bank. It was an old house with a curious bow window in front.

Mill Pond Bank.

HERBERT. All's well so far, Handel. But he's anxious to see you. (*Clara enters.*) Ah, here's Clara, here she comes.
CLARA. Pip, is it?
PIP. And you're Clara, at last! Herbert's words fail to do you justice. (*He kisses her hand.*)
CLARA. Mr. Magwitch wants to know if he may come down. Let me go fetch him. (*She goes out.*)
PIP. Herbert, she's so lovely.
HERBERT. Isn't she? I know where my good fortune lies, money or no—(*Magwitch enters.*)
MAGWITCH. I've brought you nothing but trouble, dear boy.
PIP. You're safe, that's all that matters. You know you'll have to go away?
MAGWITCH. But how—?
HERBERT. Handel and I are both skilled oarsmen—
PIP. And I've just hired a rowboat—I keep it tied up at the Temple stairs, near our rooms.
HERBERT. When the time comes, we plan to row you down-river ourselves, and smuggle you aboard a foreign packet.
PIP. Starting tomorrow I'll go rowing every day. If they see me out on the river often enough, it'll be taken as habit. If I'm out there twenty-five times, no one will blink an eye when I appear the twenty-sixth.
HERBERT. A bit of practice in the evenings won't hurt me, either. I've grown soft, cooped up in that office.
MAGWITCH. Hah. Hah! I like it—I like your plan, lads.

Throughout the following montage, Compeyson, carefully muffled, lurks here and there.

NARRATION.
Pip and Herbert went rowing the next day.

The young men, it appeared, felt a sudden urge to exercise . . .

And after the first few days, no one seemed to notice.

Pip often rowed alone, in cold, rain and sleet . . .

But no one seemed to notice.

At first he kept above Blackfriars Bridge,

But as the hours of the tide changed, he rowed further, past the tricky currents around old London Bridge.

Once he and Herbert rowed past Mill Pond Bank. They could see the house with the curious bow window from the river.

Magwitch was safe inside that house.

There seemed no cause for alarm.

But Pip knew there was cause for alarm. He could not get rid of the notion he was being watched.

Meanwhile, Pip's financial affairs began to wear a gloomy appearance, for he had vowed not to accept any more money from Magwitch, given his uncertain feelings about the man.

And as the days passed, Pip continued to think of Estella. The impression settled heavily upon him that she was married.

But he could not bear to seek out the truth of it, and clung to the last little rag of his hope.
 (*Compeyson appears directly behind him.*)
He was miserable.

And still, he could not get rid of the notion he was being watched.
 (*Pip turns around, but bumps into Mr. Jaggers, who is walking down the road.*)
JAGGERS. Mr. Pip, is it?

PIP. Mr. Jaggers.
JAGGERS. Where are you bound?
PIP. Home, I think.
JAGGERS. Don't you know?
PIP. I . . . hadn't made up my mind.
JAGGERS. You *are* going to dine, you don't mind admitting that?
PIP. I confess it, guilty of dining.
JAGGERS. And you're not engaged?
PIP. I'm quite free.
JAGGERS. Come dine with me. (*Jaggers takes his arm decisively.*) Wemmick will be joining us, too. (*Wemmick falls in with them.*)

> *Jaggers's House.*
> *Molly is serving soup from a tureen.*

JAGGERS. By the way, Miss Havisham sent you a message. She'd like to see you, a little matter of business. Will you go down?
PIP. Certainly. (*The three men sit down. Molly stands behind Jaggers's chair, silently.*)
JAGGERS. When? (*Pip glances at Wemmick, who silently mouths the word "soon".*)
PIP. I . . . soon. At once. Tomorrow. (*Wemmick nods.*)
JAGGERS. Splendid. So, Pip, your good friend, the Spider— (*To Wemmick.*)—I refer to one Bentley Drummle—appears to have played his cards well. He has won the pool, eh? (*To Wemmick.*) I refer to a young lady.
PIP. It would seem he has.
JAGGERS. Hah! He's a promising fellow in his own way, but he may not *have* it all his way. The stronger of the two will win in the end; but who is the stronger, he or she? (*He sips.*) What do you think, Wemmick?
WEMMICK. (*Shrugs.*) Here's to the Spider—what's his name?
JAGGERS. (*Lifts his glass.*) Bentley Drummle: and may the question of supremacy be settled to the lady's satisfaction. To the satisfaction of both of 'em, it never can be. (*He drinks.*) Ah, Molly, the soup is delicious this evening.
MOLLY. Thank you, master.

JAGGERS. Our Molly doesn't like company, she prefers to keep her skills for my palate alone. (*She turns her head to one side, fidgets with an apron-string. Pip suddenly stares at her. Jaggers notices.*) What's the matter, young man?
PIP. Nothing—we were speaking of a subject that's painful to me. (*Pip and Molly lock eyes for a moment. Wemmick and Jaggers attack their soup.*)
NARRATION.
The action of her fingers was not unlike that of knitting.

The look on her face was intent.

Surely Pip had seen such hands, such eyes recently.
They were fresh in his mind.

He stared at Molly's hands, her eyes, her flowing hair,
and compared them with hands, eyes, hair he knew too well.

He thought what those dearer hands might be like after
twenty years of a brutal, stormy life—

And suddenly he felt absolutely certain that this woman
was Estella's mother.

Pip managed to get through the rest of his meal as best
he could. At last, he and Wemmick thanked their host
and took to the street.
 (*Pip and Wemmick stroll. They pass Compeyson without noticing him.*)
PIP. Mr. Wemmick, we were speaking of Miss Havisham's adopted daughter at dinner. Have you ever seen her?
WEMMICK. Can't say I have. Something troubling you, Mr. Pip?
PIP. The first time I dined at Jaggers's, do you recall telling me to notice the housekeeper. A wild beast tamed, you called her.
WEMMICK. I daresay I did.
PIP. How did Mr. Jaggers tame her?
WEMMICK. We're in our private and personal capacities? (*Pip nods.*) About twenty years ago she was tried for murder at the Old Bailey, and was acquitted. Mr. Jaggers was her lawyer, of course, and I must say his defense was astonishing. The murdered person was another woman, older than Molly, and

even stronger. It was a case of jealousy. Molly was married to some sort of tramping man, and he got too familiar with the other woman. She was found dead in a barn near Hounslow Heath, all bruised and scratched — choked to death. There was no other candidate to do the murder but our Molly. — You may be sure Mr. Jaggers never pointed out how strong Molly's wrists were then. He likes to, now.
PIP. Indeed he does. How did he get her off?
WEMMICK. Molly was also suspected of killing her own child by this man of hers, to revenge herself on him. Jaggers told the jury that they were really trying her for that crime; and since there was no child, no body, no trace of a child or a body, they had no proof. I tell you, he got the jury so confused that they capitulated and acquitted her of killing her rival. She's been in his service ever since.
PIP. Do you remember the sex of the child?
WEMMICK. Said to have been a little girl, around three.
PIP. Goodnight, Mr. Wemmick, we part here. (*They go off separately. Compeyson follows Pip.*)

Havisham's.

NARRATION.
The following morning Pip journeyed down to Miss Havisham.

There hung about her an air of utter desolation,

An expression, almost, of fear.
HAVISHAM. Thank you for coming. I want to show you I'm not all made of stone. What do you wish me to do for Herbert Pocket?
PIP. I had hoped to buy him a partnership in the firm of Clarriker and Company. He's worked successfully there for the past year or so.
HAVISHAM. How much money do you need?
PIP. Nine hundred pounds.
HAVISHAM. If I give it to you, will you keep my part in it as secret as your own?

PIP. Faithfully. It would ease my mind about that, at any rate.
HAVISHAM. Are you so unhappy?
PIP. I'm far from happy—but I've got other causes of disquiet than any you know.
HAVISHAM. Pip? Is my only service to you to be this favor for young Pocket? Can I do nothing for you yourself?
PIP. Nothing, Miss Havisham. (*She takes pen, paper, writes a note.*)
HAVISHAM. This is an authorization to Jaggers to pay Clarriker nine hundred pounds to advance your friend. (*He takes the paper.*)
PIP. I thank you with all my heart. (*She takes another paper, writes.*)
HAVISHAM. Pip, here is my name. If you can ever write "I forgive her" under it, even after my death, it would mean so much . . .
PIP. Oh, Miss Havisham, I can do that now. I want forgiveness myself too much to be bitter with you. (*He reaches for her hand, but she drops suddenly to her knees, sobbing.*)
HAVISHAM. What have I done, what have I done?
PIP. I'd have loved her under any circumstances. Is she married?
HAVISHAM. She is. What have I done? What have I done?
PIP. I assure you, Miss Havisham, you may dismiss me from your conscience. Estella is a different case.
HAVISHAM. I meant to save her from a misery like my own! I stole her heart and put ice in its place.
PIP. Better to have left her a natural heart, even if it were to break.
HAVISHAM. What have I done, what have I done?
PIP. Whose child was she? (*She shakes her head.*) You don't know? But Mr. Jaggers brought her here?
HAVISHAM. I asked him to find me a little girl whom I could rear and love and save from my own fate. One night, a few months later, he brought her . . . she was fast asleep. I called her Estella. She was about three.
PIP. Good night, Miss Havisham. And thank you for your kindness to Herbert. (*He kisses her hand, goes.*)
NARRATION.
Twilight was closing in.

Pip went into the ruined garden, and roamed past the
place where he and Herbert had had their fight . . .

Past the spot where she had kissed him . . .

Past the little pot of flowers whose fragrance she
had once inhaled . . .

He turned to look at the old house once more—

When suddenly he saw a great, towering flame spring
up by Miss Havisham's window,

And he saw her running, shrieking, with a whirl of flame
blazing all about her, soaring high above her head.
  (*Screams. Fire.*)

Pip raced back into the house, tore off his great-
coat, and wrapped her in it,

Beating out the flames with his bare hands.
  (*Screams. Then they subside. Silence.*)
HAVISHAM. What have I done . . . what have I done . . .
Pip, Pip . . . forgive me . . . please, God forgive me. . . .
(*Darkness.*)

  The Temple.
  Pip lies on the sofa, Herbert is dressing his burnt hands.

HERBERT. Steady, Handel, dear boy.
PIP. You are the best of nurses.
HERBERT. The right hand's much better today. The left was
pretty badly burned, it will take more time—
PIP. Time.
HERBERT. Steady on! I saw Magwitch last evening. He sends
his love.
PIP. And how is Clara?
HERBERT. Taking good care of him. She calls him
Abel—she'll miss him when he goes.
PIP. She's such a darling. You'll be marrying soon, won't you?
HERBERT. (*Grins.*) How can I respectably care for her other-
wise? Now, this bandage will have to come off gradually, so you

won't feel it. (*He works on it.*) You know what, Handel? Old Magwitch has actually begun to grow on me.

PIP. Yes. I used to loathe him, but that's gone. Don't you think he's become more gentle? (*Herbert nods.*)

HERBERT. He told me the story of his "missus" the other night, and a wild, dark tale it is. Ah, the bandage is off most charmingly. Now for the clean, cool one.

PIP. Tell me about his woman.

HERBERT. She was a jealous one, vengeful to the last degree.

PIP. What last degree?

HERBERT. Murder — am I hurting you? (*Pip shakes his head.*) She was tried and acquitted. Jaggers defended her, that's how Magwitch first came to learn of him. — Is the bandage too tight?

PIP. It is impossible to be gentler. Pray, go on.

HERBERT. This woman had a child by Magwitch, on whom he doted. After she killed her rival, she told Magwitch she would also kill their child. There, the arm's nicely done up. You're sure you're all right? You look so pale.

PIP. Did she kill the child?

HERBERT. She did.

PIP. Magwitch thinks she did. Herbert, look at me.

HERBERT. I do look at you, dear boy.

PIP. Touch me — I've no fever? I'm not delirious?

HERBERT. You seem rather excited, but you're quite yourself.

PIP. I know I'm myself. And the man we have been hiding in Mill Pond Bank, Abel Magwitch, is Estella's father!

Jaggers's Office.

NARRATION. Pip was seized with a feverish need to verify the truth of it. As soon as he was able to leave his bed he visited Mr. Jaggers. (*Jaggers and Wemmick are busy with paperwork. Pip walks in, hands Jaggers a note.*)

JAGGERS. And the next item, Wemmick, will be — (*He sees Pip.*) What's this? (*Reads.*) An authorization signed by the late Miss Havisham . . . nine hundred pounds, payable to the firm of Clarriker and Company, Ltd., on behalf of . . . Herbert

Pocket? This must be your doing, Pip. I'm sorry we do nothing for you.
PIP. She was kind enough to ask. I told her no.
JAGGERS. I shouldn't have told her that, but every man knows his own business.
WEMMICK. Every man's business is portable property.
PIP. I did ask her for information, however . . . regarding her adopted daughter. She obliged, and I now know more about Estella than she does herself. I know her mother.
JAGGERS. Her mother?
PIP. And so do you — she cooked your breakfast this morning.
JAGGERS. (*Unperturbed.*) Did she?
PIP. But I know more, perhaps, than even you do. I also know Estella's father. (*Jaggers looks up, surprised.*)
JAGGERS. You know her father?
PIP. His name is Magwitch. He . . . lives in Australia.
JAGGERS. On what evidence does he make this claim?
PIP. He doesn't make it at all — he doesn't even know his daughter is alive.
NARRATION. Then Pip told Jaggers all he knew, and how he knew it. For once the lawyer was at a loss for words.
JAGGERS. (*Pause.*) Hah! — Where were we, Wemmick?
PIP. You cannot get rid of me so easily. I must confirm the truth from you. Please. (*Jaggers doesn't respond.*) Wemmick, you are a man with a gentle heart. I've seen your pleasant home and your old father; I know your kind and playful ways. Please, on my behalf, beg him to be more open with me —
JAGGERS. What's this?! Pleasant home? Old father?!
WEMMICK. So long as I leave 'em at home, what's it to you, sir?
JAGGERS. Playful ways?!! (*To Pip.*) This man must be the most cunning impostor in London.
WEMMICK. It don't interfere with business, does it? I shouldn't be surprised if, when you're finally tired of all this work, you plan a pleasant home of your own!
JAGGERS. Me?!
PIP. The truth, I beg you —
JAGGERS. Well, well, Pip, let me put a case to you. Mind, I admit nothing.
PIP. I understand.

JAGGERS. Put the case that a woman under such circumstances as you have named hid her child away, and only her lawyer knew where. Put the case that, at the same time, this lawyer held a trust to find a child for an eccentric, rich client, a lady, to adopt.
PIP. Yes, yes.
JAGGERS. Put the case that this lawyer lived in an atmosphere of evil. He saw small children earmarked for destruction; he saw children whipped, imprisoned, transported, neglected, hounded, cast out — qualified in all ways for the hangman. And he saw them grow up and be hanged. And always, always, he was helpless to intervene. Put the case that here was one pretty little child out of the heap that he could save. Put the case that the child grew up and married for money. That the natural mother was still living. That the father and mother, unknown to each other, were living within so many miles, furlongs, yards, if you will, of one another. That the secret was still a secret . . . until one day *you* got hold of it. Now tell me, for whose sake would you reveal the secret? (*Pause. Pip shakes his head.*) Now, Wemmick, where were we when Mr. Pip came barging in?

The Temple.

NARRATION. The next evening, Herbert came home from the office bubbling with joy, for Clarriker had offered him —
HERBERT. (*Rushing in.*) — A partnership! Think of it! We're establishing a branch office in the East Indies and I — I am to go out and take charge of it! I'll be able to take Clara and — it's a miracle! Are you surprised? No, of course not, you've always had more faith in me than I had in myself. But my dear Handel, after your commitment to Magwitch is over, perhaps . . . have you given any thought to your own future?
PIP. I'm afraid to think further than our project.
HERBERT. You might think of a future with me — I mean with Clarriker's, for in the East Indies we'll need a —
PIP. — A clerk?
HERBERT. Yes, a clerk. But Handel, you could expand into a partnership soon enough — look at me! Clara and I have talked

it over—she worries about you too, the darling. You're to live with us. We get along so well, Handel. . . . (*Pip, deeply moved, hugs him.*)
PIP. Not yet. Not for a while. After we've seen our project through there are some other things I must settle.
HERBERT. When you are ready, then?
PIP. When I am ready. And thank you.
NARRATION. That same evening, Pip received a message.
WEMMICK. Burn this as soon as you read it. Be ready to move your cargo out on Wednesday morning. J. Wemmick.
HERBERT. Wednesday!
PIP. We can be ready. Will you warn Magwitch?
HERBERT. I'll visit Clara tonight. But your burns haven't healed yet—I can tell your arm still hurts.
PIP. I shall be ready.

NARRATION.
Tuesday.

One of those March mornings when the sun shines hot and the wind blows cold . . .

Summer in the sun, winter in the shade.

The plan:
    (*Pip and Herbert pore over a map.*)
PIP. The tide turns at nine tomorrow morning—it's with us until three.
HERBERT. Just six hours.
PIP. We'll have to row into the night, anyway.
HERBERT. Where do we board the big ship?
PIP. Below Gravesend—here. See, the river's wide, there, and quite deserted. The packet ship to Hamburg passes at midnight.
HERBERT. Wemmick has booked two passages to Hamburg. The two passengers are expected to make an . . . unconventional boarding, to say the least. (*They smile at each other. Compeyson lurks on the sidelines.*)
NARRATION.
Wednesday.

The relief of putting the plan into action was enormous. The two young men set out in their boat as was their habit.

Pip felt sure they went undetected.

They soon passed old London Bridge, then Billingsgate Market, with its oyster-boats.

The White Tower.

Traitor's Gate.

Now they were among the big steamers from Glasgow and Aberdeen.

Here, at their moorings, were tomorrow's ships for Rotterdam and Le Havre.

And there stood the packet scheduled to leave for Hamburg later that evening. Pip and Herbert rowed past it with pounding hearts.

Finally they touched the little dock at Mill Pond Bank,

Where a man dressed as a river pilot was waiting. He climbed into the boat.
MAGWITCH. Dear boy, faithful boy, thankee. And thankee, Pip's companion.
NARRATION. Herbert and Pip rowed their cargo back out on the river.
MAGWITCH. If you know'd, dear boy, what it is to sit alonger my boy in the open air, arter having been kept betwixt four walls . . .
PIP. I think I know the delights of freedom.
MAGWITCH. No, you'd have to have been under lock and key to know it equal to me.
PIP. If all goes well you'll be free again within a few hours.
MAGWITCH. I hope so. But we can no more see to the bottom of the next few hours than we can to the bottom of this river. Nor yet can we hold back time's tide than I can hold this water . . . see how it runs through my fingers and is gone?
NARRATION.
The air felt cold and damp.

Pip's hands throbbed with pain.

In mid-afternoon the tide began to run strong against them, but they rowed and rowed until the sun set.

Night.

They passed Gravesend at last, and pulled into a little cove. They waited. Magwitch smoked his pipe.

They spoke very little.

Once Pip thought he heard the lapping of oars upon the water, and the murmur of voices—but then there was nothing.

He credited it to exhaustion and the pain in his hands.

They continued to wait silently by the river bank.

Then—they heard an engine! The packet for Hamburg was coming round the bend—even in the dark Pip thought he could see the smoke from her stacks!
PIP. Yes, here she comes!
HERBERT. She's slowing down—start rowing!
NARRATION.
They eased out on the river again, and headed toward the packet steamer—

—When suddenly, a four-oared galley shot out from the bank, toward them—

—On board were four oarsmen and two other figures. One held the rudder lines, and seemed to be in charge—

—The other figure sat idle: he was cloaked and hidden.

The galley began pulling up fast toward Pip's boat—

While Pip and Herbert rowed furiously toward the packet.
VOICE FROM GALLEY. You have a returned convict there—that man in the pilot's coat. His name is Abel Magwitch. I call upon him to surrender, and you others to assist!
NARRATION.
With a mighty thrust, the galley rammed Pip's small boat.
      (*Sound of wood on wood, cries, water.*)
Magwitch stood in the boat and leaned across, yanking the cloak from the other man's face.

MAGWITCH. Compeyson!
COMPEYSON. Yes, it's Compeyson.
VOICE FROM GALLEY. Surrender!
MAGWITCH. You shan't get away with it, not again, not this time!
VOICE FROM GALLEY. To starboard, to starboard—look out—
COMPEYSEN. Help, he's got hold of me—he's pulling me—overboard. . . . help!—
VOICE FROM GALLEY. We're going to capsize—watch—(*Screaming. The packet sounds its horn, thrashing in water.*) My God, the steamer! The steamer's upon us! Help—the steamer—headed toward us—(*The packet horn blows with increasing insistance. Shouts, cries, screams, splintering wood.*)
PIP. Magwitch . . . ! (*Then silence. The lapping of water.*)
NARRATION.
As the confusion abated, they saw Magwitch swimming ahead. He was hauled on board and manacled at the wrists and ankles. He had sustained severe injuries to the chest and head.

There was no sign of Compeyson.

Magwitch told his captors they had gone down together, locked in each other's arms.

After a fierce underwater struggle, only Magwitch had found the strength to swim to the surface.

Pip, shivering and wet, took his place beside the wounded, shackled creature.
MAGWITCH. Dear boy . . . I'm quite content. I've seen my boy. Now he can . . . be a gentleman without me . . .
PIP. I will never stir from your side. Please God, I will be as true to you as you have been to me.
NARRATION. Magwitch was removed to the prison hospital, but was too ill to be committed for immediate trial. Pip tried to think what peace of mind he could bring to the wounded man.
PIP. His money—his property—
JAGGERS. —It will all be forfeit to the crown, Pip. I'm sorry.
PIP. I don't care, for myself. But for mercy's sake, don't let him

know it's lost. It would break his heart if he thought I weren't to have it.
JAGGERS. You let it slip through your fingers. Poor Pip.
WEMMICK. When I think of the sacrifice of so much portable property! Your creditors will be after you now, I fear.
JAGGERS. However, I'll say nothing to Magwitch. Poor Pip. I'm late to court.
NARRATION. (*Voices echo:*) Late to court. Late to court. Late to court.

The Prison Hospital.
Magwitch lies on a mattress. Pip enters.

MAGWITCH. Dear boy, I thought you was late.
PIP. It's only just time. I waited by the gate.
MAGWITCH. Thankee, dear boy. You never desert me.
PIP. Are you in much pain today?
MAGWITCH. I don't complain of none.
PIP. You never do complain. (*A prison doctor looks at Magwitch, shakes his head.*) Magwitch, I must tell you now, at last — can you understand what I say? (*Magwitch nods.*) You had a child once, whom you loved and lost? (*Magwitch nods.*) She lived. She lives, and has powerful friends. She is a lady, and very beautiful. And I love her! (*Magwitch kisses Pip's hand. He dies.*)
PIP. Oh Lord, be merciful to him, a sinner. (*Darkness.*)

The Temple.
Pip lies sleeping on a sofa.

NARRATION.
Now Pip was all alone.

Miss Havisham and Magwitch were dead.

And Herbert had left for the Far East.

Pip should have been alarmed by the state of his financial affairs, for he was heavily in debt —

— But that he scarcely had the strength to notice.

For he was ill, very ill with fever.

He dreamed he was rowing, endlessly rowing.

He dreamed that Miss Havisham called to him from inside a great furnace.

>   (*Creditors begin carrying off the rug, a chair, etc. In the end there is only the sofa and one chair.*)

He dreamed he was a brick in the wall—

The steel beam of a vast engine.

He dreamed that the creditors had carried off all his furniture but a bed and a chair—

And that Joe was seated in the chair.

He dreamed he asked for a cooling drink, and that the beloved hand that gave it to him was Joe's.

He dreamed he smelled Joe's pipe.

And finally, one day he took courage and woke up.
PIP. Is it . . . Joe?
JOE. Which it are, old chap.
PIP. Oh, Joe, you break my heart.
JOE. Which, dear old Pip, you and me was ever the best of friends. And when you're better—wot larks! (*Pip covers his eyes for a moment.*)
PIP. How long, dear Joe?
JOE. Which you meantersay, how long have you been ill? It's the end of May.
PIP. And you've been here all this time?
JOE. Pretty nigh. For Biddy said, "Go to him, he needs you!" And I do what she tells me. Now rest, Pip. I must write a letter to Biddy, else she'll worry.
PIP. You can write?
JOE. Biddy taught me.
NARRATION.
Pip was like a child in the hands of Joe,

Who cared for him so tenderly that Pip half-believed he *was* a child again,

And that everything that had happened to him since he left the forge was a dream.

Finally the fever was gone.

But as Pip grew stronger, Joe seemed to grow less comfortable.

JOE. Dear old Pip, old chap, you're almost come round, sir.
PIP. Ay. We've had a time together I shall never forget. I know for a while I *did* forget the old days, but—
JOE. Dear Pip . . . dear sir . . . what have been betwixt us—have been. You're better now.
PIP. Yes, Joe.
JOE. Then good night, Pip. (*He tiptoes out.*)
NARRATION. And when he awoke the next morning, Joe was gone. (*Pip finds a note on Joe's chair.*)
PIP. (*Reads.*) Sir: Not wishful to intrude, I have departed. For you are well again, dear Pip, and will do better without Joe. P.S. Ever the best of friends.
NARRATION. Enclosed with the note was a receipt for Pip's outstanding debts. Joe had paid them. (*Pip puts on his jacket, takes his hat.*)
PIP. I'll go to him—to the forge. Biddy was right, he has such pride, such honor. And Biddy—Biddy is there too. Perhaps she'll find me worthier of her than I once was. Perhaps—(*He rushes off.*)
NARRATION. The first person he encountered when he climbed off the coach was his old mentor, Mr. Pumblechook.
PUMBLECHOOK. So, young man, I am sorry to see you brought so low. Look at you, skin and bones. But I knew it! You were ever pigheaded and ungrateful. I always knew it would end badly. Lo, how the mighty are fallen! How the mighty are—
NARRATION.
—But Pip could not wait to hear the conclusion of the greeting. He headed down a country lane to the forge.

The June weather was delicious.

The sky was blue, and larks soared over the green corn.

He felt like a pilgrim, toiling homeward from a
distant land.
BIDDY. It's Pip! Dear Pip—Joe, Joe, Pip's come home! Look at you, so pale and thin.
PIP. Biddy, dear girl.
BIDDY. How did you know to come today?
PIP. Today?
BIDDY. It's our wedding day. Joe and I were married this morning! (*Pip's face falls for an instant, then he brightens. Joe appears.*)
PIP. Married. Married!
JOE. Which he warn't strong enough fur to be surprised, my dear.
BIDDY. I ought to have thought, but I was so happy—
PIP. —And so am I! It's the sweetest tonic of all. Biddy, you have the best husband in the world; and you, Joe, the best wife. She'll make you as happy as you deserve to be. (*He kisses her.*) And now, although I know you've already done it in your hearts, please tell me you forgive me.
JOE. Dear old Pip, God knows as I forgive you, if I have anything to forgive.
BIDDY. Amen. (*He embraces them both.*)
PIP. And now, I must be off, to catch the coach to London. (*Joe and Biddy watch him go. For a moment, they look after him, arms around each other.*)

WEMMICK. Mr. Pip? I know it's a trying time to turn your mind to other matters, but—
PIP. —What? Anything, Wemmick.
WEMMICK. Tomorrow is only Tuesday . . . still, I'm thinking of taking a holiday.
PIP. Are you? That's very nice . . . ?
WEMMICK. I'd like you to take a walk with me in the morning, if you don't object.
PIP. Of course not. Delighted.
NARRATION.
The next morning early, after fortifying themselves
with rum-and-milk and biscuits, they did take a walk,
to Camberwell Green.

Pip was puzzled.
WEMMICK. Halloa! Here's a nice little church. Let's go in.
NARRATION. And they went in.
WEMMICK. Halloa! Here's a couple of pairs of nice gloves. Let's put them on. (*They do so. The Aged Parent and Miss Skiffins [still in her green gloves] appear with a clergyman.*) Halloa! Here is Miss Skiffins. Let's have a wedding. All right, Aged P?
AGED PARENT. All right, John!
CLERGYMAN. Who giveth this woman to be married to this man? (*No response.*) Who giveth this woman to be married to this man?
WEMMICK. (*Shouts.*) Now, Aged P. You know, "who giveth."
AGED PARENT. I do! I do! I do! All right, John?
NARRATION. And so Mr. Wemmick and Miss Skiffins were wed, with Pip as witness. (*All kiss the bride.*)
WEMMICK. (*To Pip.*) Altogether a Walworth sentiment, you understand?
PIP. I understand. Private and personal, not to be mentioned in the office.
WEMMICK. If Mr. Jaggers knew of this, he might think my brain was softening. (*The Aged nods. They all nod.*)

NARRATION.
Within a month Pip had left England. Within two he was a clerk in the Far Eastern branch of Clarriker and Pocket.

Three years later he was promoted to associate director of that branch.

For many years Pip lived happily with Herbert and Clara Pocket. When at last he returned to England, he hurried to the little village and the forge.

The Forge Kitchen. Joe sits smoking. Biddy sews. There is a small boy with a slate on Pip's old stool. Pip gazes for a moment, then enters. They embrace him. He picks up the child.

JOE. We giv' him the name of Pip for your sake, dear old boy, and hope he may grow a little like you.
PIP. You must lend him to me, once I get settled.
BIDDY. No, you must marry and get your own boy.
PIP. So Clara tells me, but I don't think so . . .
BIDDY. (*Pause.*) You haven't forgotten her.
PIP. I've forgotten nothing that ever meant anything to me. But that poor dream has all gone by, dear Biddy, all gone by.

Miss Havisham's Garden.

NARRATION. The next evening Pip's steps led him to Miss Havisham's gate. There was no house left, only ruins and a garden overgrown by weeds. (*A figure moves from the shadows toward him.*)
PIP. Estella!
ESTELLA. I wonder you know me, Pip. I've changed.
PIP. How is —
ESTELLA. My husband is dead.
PIP. I'm sorry.
ESTELLA. Don't be. He used me with great cruelty. It is over.
PIP. How strange we should meet here, where we first met.
ESTELLA. (*Pause.*) You do well?
PIP. I work pretty hard, so I do well enough. I want so little.
ESTELLA. I have often thought of you. Once you said to me, "God bless you, God forgive you." Suffering has taught me what your heart used to be —
PIP. God has forgiven you, my dear.
ESTELLA. Ay. I have been bent and broken but, I hope, into a better shape. Tell me we are friends, Pip.
PIP. We are friends.
ESTELLA. And shall continue friends apart? (*He starts to speak, hesitates, nods. He bends and kisses her hand.*)
PIP. God bless you, Estella. (*She leaves through the garden gate. Pip looks around the old place. He sees the little pot of flowers, now broken and charred, but with a few blooms still growing. He picks it up, smells them, picks one and folds it into his breast pocket. He sits on the old garden bench. As he does, voices of the past rise up. They begin slow, but speed up, overlapping.*)

NARRATION. Philip Pirrip, late of this parish
And then, Pip, wot larks!
Stop, thief, stop that boy!
Be grateful, boy, for them what has brought you up by hand.
Love her, love her, love her!
Wot larks.
Coarse little monster, why don't you cry. Cry. Cry.
This young man has . . . great expectations
Wouldn't you be happier as you are?
Did you never think it could be me?
Portable property
My dear Handel
You've the arm of a blacksmith
Love her, love her, love her!
I cannot love
I've come back to you, Pip, dear boy
A wild beast tamed
Name of Magwitch
What have I done? What have I done?
Going to be a gentleman
Great expectations.
(*Pip rises.*)
Great expectations.
(*He strides out the garden door. Darkness.*)

END OF PLAY

PROPERTY PLOT

Offstage Right
Long table with lace cloth and decayed cake with mouse on line
Trunk — Pip
Hat box — Estella
Valise — Pip
Table setting — Herbert Pocket: 2 wine glasses
                                            2 plates
                                            2 sets silverware
                                            2 napkins
Table setting — Jaggers: 4 wine goblets (fancy)
                                 4 plates
                                 4 sets silverware
                                 4 napkins
                                 4 soup bowls
Prison ship manacles — Magwitch: leg irons
Handcuffs — Lieutenant
Prison blanket — Doctor
Washing in basket — Biddy
Receipt papers — Pip
2 bells: 1 for Jaggers office, 1 for Havisham's gate
Bible — Magwitch
Knife — Magwitch
Tea cup and saucer — Pumblechook
Black tray — Molly
Tea pot
Candlestick — Pip
Wine bottle — Herbert

Onstage Right
4 London chairs (fancy)
Garden bench — Estella
Sofa — Pip
Clerk's desk — Wemmick
Blanket (refined) — Pip
Rug — Pip
5 mugs
Tray for mugs

2 sherry glasses — Pumblechook
London newspaper — Pumblechook

Offstage Left
Pipe (smoking) — Magwitch
Tablecloth — Mrs. Joe
Bread — Mrs. Joe
Bread knife — Mrs. Joe
Bucket with sponge — Young Herbert
Lantern (practical) — Estella
Washstand with basin — Jaggers
Hand towel — Jaggers
Pipe (smoking) — Joe
Letter paper — Biddy
Pen — Biddy
Burlap bag — Young Pip
Knitting — Estella
Onstage Left
4 Mrs. Joe chairs (rustic)
Stool
Pewter plates — Mrs. Joe
3 glasses
Crock — Mrs. Joe
Spoon — Mrs. Joe
Gravy boat — Mrs. Joe
3 bottles: 1 port, 2 sherry — Pumblechook
          1 brandy — Young Pip
Slate and chalk — Biddy
Sewing — Biddy
Rag — Biddy
File — Young Pip
Bread loaf — Young Pip
Pork pie — Young Pip
Cheese wedge — Young Pip
Tea cup and saucer
Newspaper — Jaggers

COSTUME PLOT

ACTOR #1

Magwitch: prisoner uniform, cap, boots, shirt pants, gold vest, boots (same), cravat, gloves, coat

ACTOR #2

Pumblechook: coat, fat pad, pants, vest, watch, shirt, cravat, shoes, wig, hat

Wemmick: coat, pants, shirt (same), cravat, watch (same), shoes (same), wig, hat, gloves, gaiters, sleeve guards

Drummle: coat, (same), vest, shirt (same), cravat (same, retied), no wig

ACTOR #3

Joe: shirt, vest, pants, boots, leather apron, neck scarf, wig, handkerchief, hat, coat, ascot

Aged Parent: night shirt (over Joe), night cap with wig attached, boots (same), coat, hat, gloves

Innkeeper: cassock, ascot (over Joe, without wig)

ACTOR #4

Pip: breeches, shirt, sox, boots, apron, jacket pants, shirt (same), vest, cravat, shoes (same), spats, coat, scarf, hat, bandages, ascot

ACTOR #5

Jaggers: coat, vest, shirt, pants, shoes, watch, cravat, eyebrows

Compeyson: prisoner uniform, cap, shoes (same) black caped coat, ascot, hat

ACTOR #6

Herbert: coat, vest, pants, shirt, shoes, cravat, wig, scarf, hat

Tailor: same as Herbert, without coat & wig, add apron

Lt.: military jacket, hat, spats, baldrake, over Herbert without wig

ACTOR #7

Mrs. Joe: dress with bodice over, apron, petticoat, lace-up boots, corset, cap

Molly: dress without bodice over, apron, wig, headscarf, shoes (same)

Character at the inn: bonnet, shawl over Mrs. Joe without apron & cap

ACTOR #8

Biddy: dress, apron, petticoat, cap with curls, shoes

Clara: dress (same, add collar & yoke), lace hat, braid, shoes (same)

Barmaid: add apron over Biddy

ACTOR #9

Estella: dress, pinafore, bloomers, petticoat, hair bow, shoes dress, petticoat, wiglettes, gloves, fan, shawl, bonnet, shoes, small headress, earrings, gloves, large fringed shawl

ACTOR #10

Miss Havisham: distressed wedding dress, petticoat, shoes, wig with veil, fingerless full length lace gloves

Miss Skiffins: coat, skirt, dickie, shoes, gloves, bonnet with curls attached

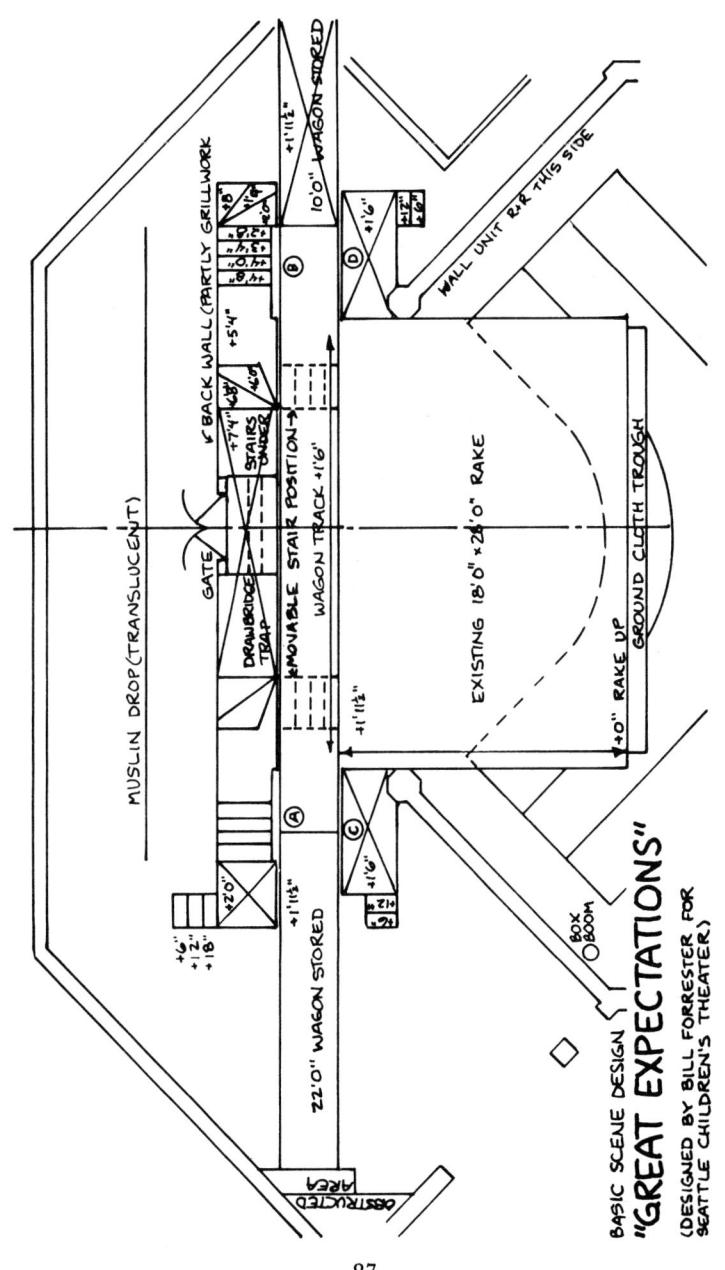

NEW PLAYS

- **SMASH by Jeffrey Hatcher.** Based on the novel, AN UNSOCIAL SOCIALIST by George Bernard Shaw, the story centers on a millionaire Socialist who leaves his bride on their wedding day because he fears his passion for her will get in the way of his plans to overthrow the British government. *"SMASH is witty, cunning, intelligent, and skillful."* –Seattle Weekly. *"SMASH is a wonderfully high-style British comedy of manners that evokes the world of Shaw's high-minded heroes and heroines, but shaped by a post modern sensibility."* –Seattle Herald. [5M, 5W] ISBN: 0-8222-1553-5

- **PRIVATE EYES by Steven Dietz.** A comedy of suspicion in which nothing is ever quite what it seems. *"Steven Dietz's ... Pirandellian smooch to the mercurial nature of theatrical illusion and romantic truth, Dietz's spiraling structure and breathless pacing provide enough of an oxygen rush to revive any moribund audience member ... Dietz's mastery of playmaking ... is cause for kudos."* –The Village Voice. *"The cleverest and most artful piece presented at the 21st annual [Humana] festival was PRIVATE EYES by writer-director Steven Dietz."* –The Chicago Tribune. [3M, 2W] ISBN: 0-8222-1619-1

- **DIMLY PERCEIVED THREATS TO THE SYSTEM by Jon Klein.** Reality and fantasy overlap with hilarious results as this unforgettable family attempts to survive the nineties. *"Here's a play whose point about fractured families goes to the heart, mind -- and ears."* –The Washington Post. *" ... an end-of-the millennium comedy about a family on the verge of a nervous breakdown ... Trenchant and hilarious ... "* –The Baltimore Sun. [2M, 4W] ISBN: 0-8222-1677-9

- **HONOUR by Joanna Murray-Smith.** In a series of intense confrontations, a wife, husband, lover and daughter negotiate the forces of passion, lust, history, responsibility and honour. *"Tight, crackling dialogue (usually played out in punchy verbal duels) captures characters unable to deal with emotions ... Murray-Smith effectively places her characters in situations that strip away pretense."* –Variety. *"HONOUR might just capture a few honors of its own."* –Time Out Magazine. [1M, 3W] ISBN: 0-8222-1683-3

- **NINE ARMENIANS by Leslie Ayvazian.** A revealing portrait of three generations of an Armenian-American family. *" ... Ayvazian's obvious personal exploration ... is evocative, and her picture of an American Life colored nostalgically by an increasingly alien ethnic tradition, is persuasively embedded into a script of a certain supple grace ... "* –The NY Post. *"... NINE ARMENIANS is a warm, likable work that benefits from ... Ayvazian's clear-headed insight into the dynamics of a close-knit family ... "* –Variety. [5M, 5W] ISBN: 0-8222-1602-7

- **PSYCHOPATHIA SEXUALIS by John Patrick Shanley.** Fetishes and psychiatry abound in this scathing comedy about a man and his father's argyle socks. *"John Patrick Shanley's new play, PSYCHOPATHIA SEXUALIS is ... perfectly poised between daffy comedy and believable human neurosis which Shanley combines so well ... "* –The LA Times. *"John Patrick Shanley's PSYCHOPATHIA SEXUALIS is a salty boulevard comedy with a bittersweet theme ... "* –New York Magazine. *"A tour de force of witty, barbed dialogue."* –Variety. [3M, 2W] ISBN: 0-8222-1615-9

DRAMATISTS PLAY SERVICE, INC.
440 Park Avenue South, New York, NY 10016 212-683-8960 Fax 212-213-1539
postmaster@dramatists.com www.dramatists.com

NEW PLAYS

- **A QUESTION OF MERCY by David Rabe.** The Obie Award-winning playwright probes the sensitive and controversial issue of doctor-assisted suicide in the age of AIDS in this poignant drama. *"There are many devastating ironies in Mr. Rabe's beautifully considered, piercingly clear-eyed work ... "* –The NY Times. *"With unsettling candor and disturbing insight, the play arouses pity and understanding of a troubling subject ... Rabe's provocative tale is an affirmation of dignity that rings clear and true."* –Variety. [6M, 1W] ISBN: 0-8222-1643-4

- **A DOLL'S HOUSE by Henrik Ibsen, adapted by Frank McGuinness.** Winner of the 1997 Tony Award for best revival. *"New, raw, gut-twisting and gripping. Easily the hottest drama this season."* –USA Today. *"Bold, brilliant and alive."* –The Wall Street Journal. *"A thunderclap of an evening that takes your breath away."* –Time. *"The stuff of Broadway legend."* –Associated Press. [4M, 4W, 2 boys] ISBN: 0-8222-1636-1

- **THE WAITING ROOM by Lisa Loomer.** Three women from different centuries meet in a doctor's waiting room in this dark comedy about the timeless quest for beauty -- and its cost. *"... THE WAITING ROOM ... is a bold, risky melange of conflicting elements that is ... terrifically moving ... There's no resisting the fierce emotional pull of the play."* – The NY Times. *"... one of the high points of this year's Off-Broadway season ... THE WAITING ROOM is well worth a visit."* –Back Stage. [7M, 4W, flexible casting] ISBN: 0-8222-1594-2

- **MR. PETERS' CONNECTIONS by Arthur Miller.** Mr. Miller describes the protagonist as existing in a dream-like state when the mind is "freed to roam from real memories to conjectures, from trivialities to tragic insights, from terror of death to glorying in one's being alive." With this memory play, the Tony Award and Pulitzer Prize-winner reaffirms his stature as the world's foremost dramatist. *"... a cross between Joycean stream-of-consciousness and Strindberg's dream plays, sweetened with a dose of William Saroyan's philosophical whimsy ... CONNECTIONS is most intriguing ... Miller scholars will surely find many connections of their own to make between this work and the author's earlier plays."* –The NY Times. [5M, 3W] ISBN: 0-8222-1687-6

- **THE STEWARD OF CHRISTENDOM by Sebastian Barry.** A freely imagined portrait of the author's great-grandfather, the last Chief Superintendent of the Dublin Metropolitan Police. *"MAGNIFICENT ... the cool, elegiac eye of James Joyce's THE DEAD; the bleak absurdity of Samuel Beckett's lost, primal characters; the cosmic anger of KING LEAR ..."* –The NY Times. *"Sebastian Barry's compassionate imaging of an ancestor he never knew is among the most poignant onstage displays of humanity in recent memory."* –Variety. [5M, 4W] ISBN: 0-8222-1609-4

- **SYMPATHETIC MAGIC by Lanford Wilson.** Winner of the 1997 Obie for best play. The mysteries of the universe, and of human and artistic creation, are explored in this award-winning play. *"Lanford Wilson's idiosyncratic SYMPATHETIC MAGIC is his BEST PLAY YET ... the rare play you WANT ... chock-full of ideas, incidents, witty or poetic lines, scientific and philosophical argument ... you'll find your intellectual faculties racing."* – New York Magazine. *"The script is like a fully notated score, next to which most new plays are cursory lead sheets."* –The Village Voice. [5M, 3W] ISBN: 0-8222-1630-2

DRAMATISTS PLAY SERVICE, INC.
440 Park Avenue South, New York, NY 10016 212-683-8960 Fax 212-213-1539
postmaster@dramatists.com www.dramatists.com